MANAGING YOUR TIME, ENERGY, AND TALENT IN MINISTRY

MANAGING YOUR TIME, ENERGY, AND TALENT IN MINISTRY

JOHN P. FLANAGAN

ST PAULS

Library of Congress Cataloging-in-Publication Data

Flanagan, John P.
    Managing your time, energy, and talent in ministry / by John P. Flanagan.
        p. cm.
    Includes bibliographical references.
    ISBN 0-8189-1233-2
    ISBN 978-0-8189-1233-7
1. Clergy—Conduct of life. I. Title.

    BV4398.F53 2006
    253'.2—dc22

                            2006007815

Scripture citations are taken from *The New American Bible*, copyright © 1987 by Catholic Bible Press, a division of Thomas Nelson Publishers, Atlanta, and used by permission. All rights reserved.

Scripture citations are taken from *The New English Bible*, copyright © 1970 by Oxford University Press, New York, and used by permission. All rights reserved.

©1999: *Parishes and Parish Ministries: A Study of Lay Ministry* by Philip J. Murnion and David DeLambo, page iii and Executive Summary, page ii. Published by the National Pastoral Life Center, 18 Bleecker Street, New York, NY 10012. www.nplc.org

Excerpts from *What Does God Want: A Practical Guide for Making Decisions*, by Rev. Michael Scanlan, T.O.R. with James Manney (Our Sunday Visitor, 1996): The permission to reproduce copyrighted materials for use was extended by Our Sunday Visitor, 200 Noll Plaza, Huntington, IN, 46750. 1-800-248-2440. Website: www.osv.com. No other use of this material is authorized.

Produced and designed in the United States of America by the Fathers and Brothers of the Society of St. Paul, 2187 Victory Boulevard, Staten Island, New York 10314-6603, as part of their communications apostolate.

ISBN: 0-8189-1233-2
ISBN: 978-0-8189-1233-7

Printing Information:

Current Printing - first digit   1   2   3   4   5   6   7   8   9   10

Year of Current Printing - first year shown

2006   2007   2008   2009   2010   2011   2012   2013   2014   2015

Dedication

I would like to dedicate this book to
the Holy Spirit
Who has continued to inspire and support me
as I struggle
to manage my time and talent in ministry
for the Greater Glory of God.

"Dum loquimur fugerit invida aetas, CARPE DIEM,
quam minimum credula postero."
Quintus Horatius Flaccus – Ode, lxil

"Even as we speak, envious time has passed, SEIZE THE DAY,
putting as little trust as possible in tomorrow."
Horace (65-67 B.C.)

CONTENTS

vii

Table of Contents

ix

ACKNOWLEDGMENTS

In writing this book I have discovered, especially as a first-time author, that it proved to be much more than a solo undertaking. In my case hundreds, perhaps thousands, of people over the years have shared with me their ideas, experiences and wisdom about their various ministries. They also frequently challenged many of my preconceived theories about ministry management. I owe a very deep debt of gratitude to these generous and dedicated servants who still labor zealously in the Lord's vineyard.

First and foremost, I would like to thank Mary Krugh for her tireless efforts and the unstinting use of her time in proofreading and typing the numerous draft manuscripts. Mary's husband, Bob Krugh, the still-disciplined Marine Corps Officer, volunteered innumerable practical suggestions. I was also most fortunate in benefitting from Karen McClelland's professional editing and insightful comments. James Frain, Edmund "Doc" Zaleski, and Eugene Miller, former college colleagues, gave me invaluable constructive criticism as well as encouragement. Rev. Msgr. Eugene J. Rebeck, my Pastor, provided me unlimited opportunities to test ministry management concepts in day-to-day parish operations. Above all I want to thank my wife, Eileen, who exhibited infinite patience and understanding when I "was on that computer and had my nose in all those books" for hours on end. Her continued support encouraged me to persevere.

I gratefully acknowledge the following individuals who so generously responded to my survey on how they managed their time and talent in the performance of their respective ministries:

David Abele, Executive Director
National Association of Catholic Family Life Ministries
Dayton, Ohio

Cindee Case, President of Board of Directors
National Catholic Young Adult Ministry Association
Youngstown, Ohio

Rev. Msgr. Joseph M. Champlin, Former Rector
Immaculate Conception Cathedral
Syracuse, New York

Deacon William T. Ditewig, Ph.D., Executive Director
Secretariat for Diaconate, U.S.C.C.B.
Washington, D.C.

Very Rev. Thomas A. Krosnicki, S.V.D., Provincial
Society of the Divine Word
Techny, Illinois

His Eminence Roger Cardinal Mahony
Archdiocese of Los Angeles
Los Angeles, California

Rev. Msgr. Thomas McGread
St. Francis of Assisi Church
Wichita, Kansas

Rev. Frank J. McNulty
Saint Teresa's Church
Summit, New Jersey

His Excellency Bishop Robert F. Morneau
Auxiliary Bishop of Green Bay
Green Bay, Wisconsin

Rev. Thomas P. Sweetser, S.J., Director
The Parish Evaluation Project
Milwaukee, Wisconsin

Rev. Damien Thompson, O.S.C.D., Abbot
Abbey of Gethsemani
Trappist, Kentucky

Sister Mary Ann Zollmann, B.V.M., Past President
Leadership Conference of Women Religious
Dubuque, Iowa

INTRODUCTION

> When I stand before God at the end of my life I would hope that not one single bit of talent is left, and I could say, "I had used everything You gave me."
>
> *Erma Bombeck*

I believe, when reflecting on our own lives, most of us would express sentiments similar to Erma Bombeck's. The only change I might add would be, "I had used everything You gave me as *effectively as possible.*"

You may be asking yourself the following questions as you begin reading this book: "How great is the need in the marketplace for such a manual for those involved in ministry?" "How will I directly benefit from reading this book?" "Why did the author write this book and what are his qualifications for doing so?" These are very valid and realistic questions so I will attempt to answer them as candidly as possible.

One of my primary objectives in this book is to enable you to experience a major *metanoia* (change of heart) *moment* which will inspire you to change or improve, in at least one way, the manner in which you are currently spending your life in ministry.

Even if you come away from this book having gained only one new insight, my efforts will have proven worthwhile. But I submit to you that you will benefit in many other ways as well, as I believe the principles and insights outlined in the following pages will demonstrate.

How Great Is the Need for This Type of Text for Those Involved in Ministry?

First, I would agree that you could find some excellent publications that will help you manage your time. But to my knowledge, there are none that attempt to address how you can *effectively* manage your time, energy, and talent *in ministry*. Many years ago I began to recognize this unique need and have tried to satisfy it by applying sound management techniques to the special and diverse vocation of ministry. Marketing professionals still offer this sage advice to aspiring entrepreneurs and those eager to enter the world of sales and marketing: "First, you must find a real need, then fill it." I think fledgling and veteran authors alike would also do well to follow this same admonition whether they are communicating information, offering solutions to problems, or affording pleasure to their prospective readers.

I am especially reminded of this responsibility to respond to readers' real needs when I walk through those mammoth Borders or Barnes & Noble bookstores. As I gaze at thousands of smartly bound and neatly stacked volumes, I realize they represent a mere fraction of the 165,000 new titles published yearly in the United States alone. "How many of these books," I ask, "will satisfy the perceived needs of potential purchasers?" The startling answer is "precious few!" Publishers will readily admit that only 15% of all books they produce will generate a profit, 40% will break even, and the remaining 45% will be financial losers. So, whether you are a publisher, author, or reader, you are generally taking a sizeable risk with your time and money. I cite these statistics because I really don't want to be guilty of contributing to that 85% of publications which might not be purchased or read. And so, for several years I kept asking myself this question: "Do clergy and laity really have an urgent need to manage their time, energy, and talent more effectively in their world of ministry?" I decided to monitor the ministry marketplace and test the need among various ministry groups.

Over a ten-year period I helped well over a hundred Catholic churches introduce Stewardship programs to their parishioners. In the process, I trained hundreds of volunteers, who in turn instructed others in giving of their time, talent, skills, and treasure to God through the Church. In almost all cases I discovered that committee members found it easier to motivate churchgoers to make financial contributions rather than giving their time, energy, and talent. The volunteers admitted they also were more comfortable doing the same. The reasons for their reluctance were interesting. Both volunteers and parishioners told me they could readily write a check or open their wallets once they recognized the church needed a new roof or the budget was woefully under-funded. Some also understood they should contribute regardless of demonstrated financial need because it was a biblical mandate to return a portion of their income to God. But their reluctance to donate time and skills to the parish often presented a formidable challenge to my efforts. When I suggested it was simply a case of their using the same skills, intelligence, time, and energy which they exercised in their respective jobs, I would get these answers: "I can't see how my skills are that relevant to parish activities"; "I really don't feel that comfortable because I am not convinced my talents are adequate"; "I'm so busy with my family needs and social activities that I can't spare time for the parish." This presented us with a dual challenge: parishioners and potential volunteers were reluctant to contribute skills and time but also felt they could not apply their gifts in the parish in a meaningful manner.

In the early years I searched everywhere for training programs that would answer these challenges. I needed a program that could educate parishioners on the theology of giving as well as a process that would help train and motivate them to contribute their talents, time, and energy in practical ways. Fortunately, I found abundant literature on the theological and scriptural rationale for Stewardship as well as excellent material on Sacrificial Offering or Treasure programs, but very little on how to implement the time- and talent-giving process. So I wrote my own programs and continue to use them in parishes. Based on this experience I validated the need to write segments of this book for the general parishioner population.

I was able to confirm the need within another community when I designed and conducted a series of seminars for parish staffs, committees, and Deacons in several dioceses. I labeled these seminars "How to Manage Your Time, Talent, and Energy for God." I frequently revised the content of those courses which then formed another section of this book. That ministry population, including clergy and lay leaders, confirmed again and again that they needed and wanted training on how to more effectively manage time and talent in their respective ministries. I was encouraged to continue the research.

I further tested my concepts and training needs when I conducted capital building campaigns for churches in several dioceses. In professional fund-raising projects you are playing for high stakes and cannot afford to fail, particularly when you are building three- to five-million dollar churches. Invariably, my biggest challenge lay not in persuading parishioners to pledge sacrificial amounts of money, but in training and motivating volunteer staffs to effectively use their unique talents and sacrifice their time to guarantee a successful campaign. Apparently my strategy worked since all the church campaigns resulted in my achieving or exceeding the goals.

Finally, I had an opportunity to evaluate the needs within my own parish. Before and after I was ordained a Permanent Deacon in 1981, I enjoyed a unique opportunity to interact with hundreds of lay leaders and parishioners as they performed their various ministries and staff duties. I was fortunate to serve in a parish, which, in many ways largely due to sound pastoral leadership, could serve as a model of good ministry management. What a blessing to be able to labor in a vineyard where I could learn, test, and validate management principles as we applied them in everyday typical parish situations. I continued to arrive at the same conclusions as I did in other parish settings. In a certain sense I hesitate to cite these situations lest it appear a bit boastful on my part. But I know you, the conscientious reader, will demand facts and proofs, and not just fanciful theories before you risk adopting new approaches in your ministry.

I believe the interest in integrating more effective management methods in ministry will continue to grow as rapidly as the number of people entering ministry. In their text, *Parishes and Parish Ministers — A Study of Lay Ministry,* Monsignor Philip J. Murnion and David De Lambo state:

> The number of lay parish ministers, i.e., religious and lay in pastoral roles... has increased 35 percent, from

21,569 in 1992 to 29,146 (of whom 20,402 are full time and 8,744 are part-time) in 1997. The lay parish ministers are to be found in 63 percent of the parishes of the country, where they had been in only 54 percent of the parishes in 1992. In 1992, 42 percent were religious and 59 percent lay; in 1997, 28.9 percent were religious and 71 percent lay. This trend toward lay people will only continue. This has important implications for education, training, and formation for parish ministry.

In its May 7, 2003 report, the Center for Applied Research in the Apostolate (CARA), states: "The biggest boom in ministerial formation in the past two decades, however, is in formation for lay ministry. When CARA first surveyed those programs in 1985-86, it found 206 programs with an enrollment of 10,500. In 2002-03 there were 313 degree- or certificate-granting programs with a combined enrollment of 35,448." These are the Lay Ecclesial Ministers, the fastest growing ministry group in the Catholic Church. The second fastest growing group is the Permanent Diaconate with 14,800 current Ordained Deacons and 2,800 in formation in the U.S. I am fairly certain, based on these validations and the growing numbers of ministers, that the need does exist for ongoing management education.

How Will I Directly Benefit From This Book?

When I speak to audiences or write an article, in my mind's eye I try to tune in to their favorite FM frequency. We all have one. For most people it's WIIFM or *what's in it for me?* Years ago a communications consultant suggested I visualize that each person in the audience has this question pasted across his forehead in big bold letters: **"What's In It For Me?"** You also

xviii

must be asking yourself the same question, especially if you intend to spend several hours reading this book. I feel that I owe you a reasonable return on your investment and so as I wrote I tried to visualize how I can help you benefit by applying these concepts to your ministry in a practical way. Following are some of the expected benefits you should experience:

Chapter 1 encourages you to become more keenly aware of the brevity of your life by responding to those precious *wake-up calls* or *metanoia moments* which can completely change the course of your life. We then learn in Chapter 2 that we are all called to the role of Stewardship which means we are mandated by Scripture to return to God a portion of our time, talent, and treasure. Chapter 3 addresses the workaholic or super-servant syndrome. I then reveal the first important *secret* of time management in ministry. I also explore the principle that requires managing one's energy if we are to effectively manage our time. Chapter 4 responds to those who may be reluctant to use professional time management techniques in their ministry. We focus on that ancient philosophical dictum: "First you must know and manage yourself before you can successfully manage your time and others." Chapter 5 outlines the "how" and "why" of setting spiritual goals. I explain how *Ministry by Objectives* follows the classic MBO or *Management by Objectives* formula. Chapter 6 illustrates how we can use the art of *Visualization* and *Priority Picking* to enhance the goal-setting process. We learn in Chapter 7 how to "log our life" in order to get an honest picture of how and where we are spending our precious hours. We identify our *Time Wasters* and finally write a daily *To-Do List* as a priority guide for our ministry activities. In Chapter 8 we talk about the *Disciples Dilemma* which describes our difficulty in delegating duties to others. We list suggestions on how to multiply our ministry through others. We are bold enough to touch on that painfully sensitive area known as "politics and envy in ministry," and we make suggestions on how to avoid those destructive demons.

All of us procrastinate, but some more than others. In Chapter 9 you may see yourself in several of the procrastination profiles, but you will also learn how you can do something about these habits of delay, now. I demonstrate in Chapter 10 how you can escape the *Activity Trap* by using the famous 80/20 rule to your advantage. I reveal in Chapter 11 how you can save two hours a day and how some secrets of the saints may help you. You will be greatly surprised to observe how you really can save at least two hours a day from your current routine in areas of computer use, TV watching, commuting, reading, meeting activities, and countless other areas of your life and ministry. Chapter 12 will reinforce those ancient words of wisdom, "There is a time for everything." In the words of Fr. Joseph Champlin, Former Rector of the Immaculate Conception Cathedral, Syracuse, New York: "There will always be time enough for the truly important things in our lives." In the final chapter we reveal the second major *secret* for using your time effectively in ministry and then dispel the myth that "There is Time Enough" to make all the important changes that are required in our lives… since that time is **now!** We end this final chapter with these words of hope which assures us in the truest scriptural sense that "all things are possible" when we do the will of God.

Why Did I Write This Book and What Qualifies Me to Do So?

I wrote this book because I really believed I had something very important to tell my audience. I sensed a growing passion to share, and this compulsion would not go away. Writing this book took longer than I had anticipated but it needed time for testing. I take some comfort in learning that the popular novelist Stephen King was in the process of writing his book, *The Dark Tower*, over the course of twenty-five years. I also took many years in both validating and writing these various ministry management principles before daring to share them with you in this book.

There is a tablet dating back to 2800 B.C. that was unearthed several years ago in Babylon. The writing on it reflected some major concerns of people who lived forty-eight centuries ago but, curiously, are still of concern to people today. That inscription revealed, "The world must be coming to an end. Children no longer obey their parents, *and every man wants to write a book.*" Perhaps the world has really not changed that much after all. I suppose many people at one time or another have had the innate desire to share their lives and experiences with others in written form. I am one of just such a group because I had a growing compulsion to write about experiences and some lessons learned in ministry that just possibly might help others.

I believe my major moment of motivation occurred the day we finally completed a five-year project for one of the largest insurance companies in the U.S. I was then the Director of Licensing, Product and Sales Training for over 25,000 life insurance agents and was preparing them to enter the Property and Casualty insurance market. About the same time I was accepted into the training program for the Permanent Diaconate. My own *metanoia moment* occurred when I realized I had spent many years, along with countless other colleagues, using my time and talents to help make millions for my company, "A

Piece of the Rock" (the advertising slogan used by my employer at that time). And now I knew I would be working for "The Rock," which is the Church, and could confidently transfer some of those marketing and management skills to my new life in ministry.

By no means do I profess to be proficient in all the dimensions of management, but I do know I have made progress in some areas while continuing to struggle in many others. Lessons learned through 45 years in the business community as well as 25 years of Diaconal duties helped form a practical framework for me in composing this text. Real-life anecdotes are included from my own life, as well as the lives of others, to lend credibility to the message. I have left to other authors, past and future, the treatment of those other important areas of management such as controlling, budgeting, accounting, communicating, motivating, and implementing. Finally, it is my fond hope that our readers will not subscribe to the Author and Professor Emeritus of University of South Alabama Louis E. Boone's facetious observation, "I am definitely going to take a course in time management... just as soon as I can work it into my schedule." If you have read this far I feel confident you have already decided to "work it into your schedule," and also work it into your life of ministry.

Chapter One

THE SHORTNESS OF TIME

Lord, let me know my end, the number of my days,
That I may learn how frail I am.
You have given my days a very short span;
My life is nothing before you,
All mortals are but a breath.
I know you have made my days a mere span long.
Psalm 39:4-5

Tempus irreparabile fugit.
(Time flies, never to return.)
Publius Virgilius Maro (70-19 B.C.)

Life Is Brief, Time Is Short, Time Is Life

A doctor was addressing a group of recovering alcoholics and decided to demonstrate the devastating effects of alcohol on one's brain. He filled a glass full of water and then dropped in a fishing worm. The little creature swam around and eventually crawled out. The doctor then pulled a flask of bourbon from his hip pocket and emptied it into another glass. He dropped in the worm, held the glass up for all to see, and the poor worm began to dissolve before their very eyes. "There," he announced, "what's the moral of that demonstration?" A very

1

inebriated voice from the rear of the room shouted, "Doc, that tells me that if you drink enough alcohol you'll never have worms."

As you read this book you will be inclined to analyze the concepts and interpret the principles based on your own background and experience. That is normal and part of the learning dynamic. You may see "worms" in some of the suggested examples or theories. I only ask that you keep an open mind and then select those solutions that may help you more effectively manage your special talents and time in ministry.

As we begin, take a moment now to recall just one event or incident that made you make a major change in your life. It may have been the death of a family member, meeting the young man or woman whom you later married, a near-death experience, a profound religious encounter, a war-combat engagement, job change, or perhaps what seemed at the time to be only a minor occurrence. Any one of these may have produced a surprisingly dramatic difference in your life.

I believe we all have major moments and defining events in our lives that force us to quickly face our own mortality. We then realize, often in a profound way, how precious our time really is and how suddenly our life can end. Unfortunately, for some, these events are only passing phenomena and are soon forgotten. But, for those of us who really care, these events present unique opportunities to make positive changes in our lives. Look at these major markers in our lives as *metanoia moments* or rare windows of opportunity to turn our lives completely around.

I feel we are experiencing major moments of grace when we recognize how pitifully brief our span of life can be and how quickly it can vanish. But our most significant insights may occur when we recognize the overwhelming need to do more for God and neighbor in the remaining years God may give us.

A Wake-Up Call

> Return, you humans, to dust,
> saying, "return you mortals."
> Before a watch passes in the night,
> you have brought them to their end;
> They disappear like sleep at dawn;
> they are like grass that dies.
> It sprouts green in the morning;
> By evening it is dry and withered.
> Psalm 90:5-6

We were trapped on the sixth floor of the tallest building in Lynbrook, Long Island, while the fire raged throughout the floors below us. It was May 1970. I had just helped a sixty-five-year-old business acquaintance and his eight female employees crawl out onto the huge fire ladder. I then stepped out on the ledge. The firemen had already evacuated the occupants of the other floors but for some unknown reason they bypassed our floor. Finally, our frantic cries for help alerted the fire fighters to our desperate situation. As they began escorting the terrified women down the ladder, I heard the Captain's voice shouting to me over the bull horn: "You, at the top, get off the ladder now, it's buckling from the weight." I actually considered leaping from that window ledge in the false hope that the firemen would be able to catch me. Desperation does indeed distort one's reason.

I reluctantly re-entered the smoke-filled room and immediately began gagging and heaving. I sensed asphyxiation had begun. I cried out, "Lord, I'm too young to die — I want to see my wife and children again — I have so many more things I want to do — and I will change my life. Please Lord, just give me one more chance to live and I will make it up to you."

These were the all-too-familiar pleas of a man bargaining with God when he is at death's door. Just as I was fading into unconsciousness, I vaguely realized that some firemen were smashing down the door. They clamped an oxygen mask over my face and carried me down the stairs, then out into fresh air and to glorious freedom.

Did I keep my promise to God and make meaningful changes in my life? Well, yes, and no. It would take several more years and numerous wake-up calls before I completely re-directed my life. How I marvel at those courageous people who quickly respond to the lightning bolt of grace that frequently accompanies a traumatic event. They seem to recognize the true brevity of life and dramatically change their lives forever. But for most of us the Lord of the Second Chance must call again and again before we seriously listen. God gives us all so many second chances. Many of us fail to recognize them or choose to ignore them. Reminders of our fragile mortality fill our everyday lives. Think about your own life. It can be a near-death experience, the sudden demise of a family member or acquaintance, a sudden illness or an accident that shocks you into recognizing how slender is the tether that connects you to your earthly life.

I happen to love birthdays. They represent another year of survival and possibly growth in wisdom. The downside is that they seem to arrive more rapidly as we age. We quickly do the arithmetic and just as quickly try to distract our minds with more pleasant matters. Birthdays and anniversaries give us signs and signals that there are so many things we still want to

4

do, but will not have time to accomplish them. Over time we may become somewhat immune to these signals. This can be especially true for those in ministry. We become so involved in other people's problems, sufferings, and deaths that our ears are deafened to those bells of eternity as they summon other souls. But those signal bells are also tolling for us.

Perhaps you are reading this book because you have finally decided to do something about how you manage your time and your life. You may be involved in full time ministry, or are devoting only several hours a week in service to God, or have just started a ministry project. No matter what your situation might be, I can only hope this book will make you more receptive to the many *wake-up* calls God is placing in your life. You know you can't escape this reality — your life is brief and your time so pitifully short. But you should rejoice and take heart, my friends, because there is so much you can do to change. The encouraging news is that there is still some time.

The Importance of Time

> I tell you, brothers, the time is running out.
> 1 Corinthians 7:29

"Time for me is now much more important than money or material things," replied a former executive and longtime friend when I asked him how he was spending his retirement. He echoed the sentiment of millions, at least those who had the wisdom to recognize the value of time. I might add that the gift of time has always been more important than money and possessions regardless of one's age. How regrettable it is that we come to realize it only later in life.

5

So precious is this gift of time that those who recognize its real value will react in remarkably different ways in trying to use or conserve it. Queen Elizabeth I allegedly insisted on standing while in the process of dying, and then gasped, "I will give all my possessions, but for one more moment of time." She was so fearful of death that she clung desperately to those final fleeting moments of her life. It is not that uncommon, in the various stages of death, for some to bargain forcefully with God.

I remember ministering to a middle-aged owner of a large factory when he was in the last stages of lung cancer. During my last visit, Jim whispered in a hoarse voice, "But John, I just need more time to spend with my family and to settle my business — there are just too many loose ends in my life." He then grabbed me by the shirt and pleaded, "Please tell me honestly that there is a life hereafter for me, otherwise my life has been wasted." Countless souls suffer through a similar terror. But we need not have this same regrettable experience. We can best prepare for a happy death by living as though each minute, hour, and day is the most important and most precious gift from God.

Michel de Montaigne, the French philosopher, makes that significant point in his essay "To Study Philosophy Is to Learn to Die." He wrote: "The utility of living consists not in the length of days, but in the use of time; a man may have lived long, and yet lived but a little." Another philosopher advised, "Treat each day as your last, and one day you will be right."

Time is important because, like gold and other precious metals, it is in relatively short supply. "For the Man who made time made mountains of it" reads an ancient Irish proverb. It just seems that way at times, for we all have exactly the same 24 hours a day and 168 hours a week, but it is still never enough.

Some advertising gurus will claim that certain services and products will "give" or "save" us minutes or even hours. Actually, those labor- and time-saving devices may reduce the time ordinarily required to perform a task by freeing up that time to be used for other pursuits. The irony is that maintaining these devices may eat up most of the time we "save" or we may simply fritter away those saved hours in useless activities.

We can't increase the number of hours in a day. We can, however, learn to use our available hours more effectively. We can't purchase more hours at Wal-Mart, bank them at Chase Manhattan, or store them on a Gateway computer. We can only spend, abuse, or lose them. This gift of time is so very precious and important because it is irrevocable, irreversible, and irreplaceable.

Clockmakers for centuries were fond of attaching an hourglass and eagle wings to the bonnets of their most expensive masterpieces. At the base of the timepiece they inscribed Virgil's familiar Latin phrase, "Tempus Fugit," Time Flies. But the famous Roman poet actually penned, "Time flies, never to return," thus adding a more ominous note to that age-old reminder.

It's how we use our time that makes all the difference. Did you ever wonder how many successful people seem to achieve so much more in their lives than you do? We know and admire them. Many serve God and others in extraordinary ways. It's true, some differ in their talent and energy levels but, like you and I, they all have the same twenty-four hours a day. What then are their secrets? That's what this book is about. I will be revealing those *secrets* or principles that made a difference in their lives and can do the same in yours.

The Final-Five Phenomenon

Perhaps those of you who are more knowledgeable about football can explain what I call "The Football Final-Five Phenomenon." You have witnessed it countless times, I'm sure. It can happen when the two football teams seem to be coasting along in a boring, lackluster game. Then, during the final five or ten minutes, the game becomes a totally different contest. The losing team, suddenly and miraculously, draws on a hidden reserve of superhuman energy. Their seemingly defeated quarterback orchestrates some dazzling plays that help score one or more dramatic touchdowns. His team achieves victory in a few magical minutes. So why didn't those hulking heroes produce similar results during the first three quarters? It baffles me, but I'm sure the sports psychologists can come up with some plausible explanations. Perhaps the pain and growing embarrassment at the prospect of losing became so acute that it finally galvanized them into action.

I submit that a similar phenomenon occurs in our own lifestyle at times. Why do we risk waiting until time is running out? Why do we delay until the final quarter or the "two-minute warning" whistle blows before we finally awaken to the reality that we are playing in the Super Bowl game of life where there are no practices or make-up games?

> *Tempus fugit et nos fugimus in illus.*
> (Time flies and we fly with it.)
> Ovid (23-18 B.C.)

Chapter Two

THE ROLE OF STEWARDSHIP

The Divine Command

> As each one has received a gift,
> use it to serve one another
> as good stewards of God's varied grace.
>
> 1 Peter 4:10

We cannot adequately discuss how to manage time and talent without addressing the important role of stewardship in our lives. The word *stewardship* or *tithing* causes some Christians to feel uncomfortable. They mistakenly identify it with the act of solely giving a percentage of one's money to church or charity. Sharing one's wealth is required but represents the least important aspect of stewardship. The history of stewardship confirms that those who give generously of their talent and time also give unstintingly of their wealth.

Stewardship is a way or philosophy of life. We live a life of stewardship when we acknowledge that God has literally given us everything we have and therefore we have an obligation to return to Him, through others, a portion of those gifts. Stewardship is that constant awareness that we pass through this life but once; therefore we should use our gifts of time, talent, and treasure for the glory of God and service to others.

9

Tithing, or the concept of stewardship, is deeply rooted in both the Old and New Testaments. In fact, references to stewardship appear over two hundred-fifty times in the Bible. It is sad that many Christians erroneously believe stewardship, like ministry, is practiced only by lay people directly involved in church-related activities. The message is clear that all believers are called to practice stewardship at home, at work, and in all aspects of their lives. Although in this book I focus especially on those who are active in church ministries, everything I discuss applies equally to all who are called to stewardship.

Unique Gifts from God

> There are different kinds of spiritual gifts,
> but the same Spirit.
> There are different forms of service,
> but the same Lord.
> There are different workings
> but the same God
> who produces all of them in everyone.
>
> 1 Corinthians 4:6

The adage that "all men are created equal," as always, has to be qualified. While we all have the same number of hours in a day and the same number of days in a week, we have been given varying amounts and types of talent. We therefore will be judged according to how we have used our unique God-given gifts and talents. Those with lesser gifts are no less worthy of salvation nor necessarily any less able to work towards their salvation. It is a sobering thought to realize we are only temporary tenants on this planet. The famous composer Eddie Cantor once quipped, "Service to others is the rent we pay for our room on this planet and I'd like to be a good tenant."

Isn't it strange that princes and kings
And clowns that caper in sawdust rings,
And ordinary folk like you and me
Are builders of eternity,
To each is given a bag of tools,
An hourglass and a book of rules,
And each must build, ere life is flown,
A stumbling block or a stepping-stone.
                                    Author unknown

Whoever wishes to be great among you
will be your servant;
whoever wishes to be first among you
will be the slave of all.
For the Son of Man did not come
to be served but to serve
and to give His life as a ransom for many.
                                    Mark 10:43-45

God gives each of us certain talents to be used for His glory
and to help others. Sometimes multi-gifted stewards are
tempted to take undue credit for their talents and successes
while serving God and neighbor. We expect this attitude from
many in secular professions where boasting about one's
achievements is indeed a legitimate form of assertiveness.
However, it is unseemly in the practice of stewardship and
ministry to even appear to take undue pride in one's special
talents. Certainly we are to be commended for our dedication.
But when pride pumps us full of an inflated sense of self-
importance it is certain we will be less effective in ministry.
Sadly, it will be said of us, "Behold, they have already received
their reward."

Whatever you do,
do from the heart and for the Lord
and not for others,
Knowing that you will receive from the Lord

11

the due payment of the inheritance.
Be servants of the Lord Jesus Christ.
Colossians 3:23-24

I keep a copy of the above verse inside my Liturgy of the Hours prayer book. I refer to it time and again when I encounter occasional bureaucracy and politics as I pursue my ministry. It serves as a compass to help me direct my efforts to the only goal that really matters. It helps me concentrate on Him whom I am really serving and that is the Lord Jesus Christ and not mere men. We waste so much of our time and energy when we permit ourselves to become mired down in needless bureaucracy and especially the quicksand of political maneuvering.

Rewards of Stewardship

Try me in this, says the Lord God of hosts,
shall I not open for you the floodgates of heaven
to pour down blessings upon you without measure?
Malachi 3:10

Here are but a few of the temporal rewards we may expect to receive when we are generous with God and others:

• *Unlimited Blessings*

The prophet Malachi is referring to the generous promise God makes to us when we give to Him the first fruits of our time, talent, and treasure. Did you ever marvel why wonderful, undeserved, and unforeseen things happen to you or members of your family? Your health might have improved, you may have received a raise or promotion, or you may have been delivered from an addictive habit. I believe it is not presumptu-

12

ous to ascribe such blessings to a generous God who is rewarding His stewards for performing faithful service. And these are only the visible blessings. Can you imagine the unseen gifts and graces that God showers down upon us?

• *A Sense of Satisfaction and Fulfillment*

> Give and gifts will be given to you;
> a good measure, packed together,
> shaken down, and overflowing,
> will be poured into your lap.
> For the measure with which you measure
> will in return be measured out to you.
>
> Luke 6:38

I really believe the Creator has so programmed us that when we use our talents to help others we will experience both a natural and supernatural sense of satisfaction. When we do vigorous exercise like cycling, jogging, or swimming our metabolism releases those "feel-good" hormones called endorphins. We experience certain pleasant, satisfying feelings. In a similar way spiritual endorphins are released within us when we exercise our gifts and talents. It is not as though we seek these sensations when we do good works. It's just that God seems to reward us in this special way. Those "feel-good" sensations may give us another legitimate incentive to continue performing good works.

• *No Regrets, No Remorse*

> He is no fool who gives up what he cannot keep,
> to gain what he cannot lose.
>
> James Elliott

Shakespeare, in Act III, Scene II of *Henry VIII,* has Thomas Cardinal Wolsey recite one of literature's most poignant speeches. Wolsey, in real life, was an advisor and trusted minister to the King and apparently spent more time in the King's court than in the cathedral. He addresses Thomas Cromwell: "O Cromwell, Cromwell, had I but served my God with half the zeal I served my king, he would not in mine age have left me naked to mine enemies."

Who of us upon our deathbed will experience remorse because we dedicated our time unselfishly serving the Lord and others during our lifetime? The best preparation for death is a lifetime of faithful stewardship. We will be tremendously consoled to hear those reassuring words of Christ: "Well done, good and faithful servant."

- *Peace of Mind; Tranquility of Soul*

Have you ever gazed carefully on the face of an aged monk or nun or a very holy person? They seem to have that special aura that radiates a certain peace of soul. Their demeanor springs from an interior tranquility of spirit and bespeaks a life of service to others. They know the secret of life. Their response to the scriptural mandate of stewardship gives them that quiet assurance that they have achieved the most important purpose in life. They have enjoyed that true success denied to many of the kings, princes, presidents, and politicians of this world.

- *The Joys of His Kingdom*

> I slept and dreamed that life was joy.
> I awoke and saw that life was service.
> I acted, and behold, service was joy.
> Rabindranath Tagore

14

The faithful steward will receive even greater rewards in addition to the unlimited blessings promised by the prophet Malachi, as well as peace of mind, freedom from regret, and a sense of fulfillment. Jesus, very pointedly in the Parable of the Talents (Matthew 25:14-30), promises the industrious stewards this impressive reward: "Come. Share your master's joy." This passage has been interpreted to mean, "joy in the banquet of God's Kingdom." Prospero Grech, O.S.A., Professor of New Testament at the Augustinian Theological Faculty in Rome, writes that "Jesus never clearly defines what he means by the Kingdom of God. He takes its knowledge for granted." But we know from other scriptural passages that Christ is referring to the "joys of the banquet of heaven" as well as the joy we will experience as members of his Kingdom on earth.

In the parable of The Ten Gold Coins (Luke 19:11-28), Christ also promises to those stewards who invested their coins wisely, "I tell you, to everyone who has, more will be yours." It follows that the more effectively we use our talents, the more opportunities, the more responsibilities, and trust will be given us to progressively pursue our ministry.

Service is the Ultimate Measure of Success

> I believe the rendering of useful service
> is the common duty of mankind
> and that only in the purifying fire of sacrifice
> is the dross of selfishness consumed
> and the greatness of the human soul set free.
> John D. Rockefeller, Jr.

I believe that the faithful and effective steward is the ultimate successful person in life. There is an extensive body of business and motivational literature which defines the concept of success as it is exemplified in the world of business, entertainment, sports, military, science, and academia. The criteria for success vary somewhat for each discipline, but there is one paramount trait that is universally agreed upon to be the critical component of the success dynamic. It's called "Service." Philosophers and psychologists have long espoused the notion that for one to be truly successful he must ultimately live a life of service to his fellow beings. Business people have always realized that providing quality service to their clients is of utmost importance in producing a profit and retaining their customer base.

I once worked for a company which was experiencing major customer complaint problems. "Do something about this debacle, John," my boss commanded me one day. "And I want to see results within six months." My department spent thousands of dollars dispatching staff to attend customer relations seminars across the country and conduct exhaustive research. We eventually reversed the negative trend by producing a countrywide program that motivated our personnel to sincerely relate and respond to our customers' needs. We distilled everything we learned and taught into a single motto: "Sincerely Care About Serving People." But our customer relations philosophy was not necessarily motivated by altruism but rather by the urgent need to retain customers and produce profits for the company. Best-selling author, Stephen R. Covey, in his insightful book *The 8th Habit — From Effectiveness to Greatness,* proposes that the world is a vastly changed place and it requires that business and society adopt a new mind-set that puts service to others as its overarching purpose. He writes: "We grow more personally when we give ourselves to others ... organizations are established to serve human needs. There is no other reason for their existence." This philosophy represents a revolutionary sea change in the way businesses must begin to act if they are to survive. Robert Greenleaf, author of the *Servant Leadership* series, and more recently in *The Institution as Servant,* applies the whole concept of stewardship to organizations. I am pleased to cite these encouraging developments in the business world which is beginning to recognize the need and value of sincerely trying to meet people's needs.

In no way do I mean to diminish the value and nobility of altruistic, idealistic, or philanthropic activities, but I believe our service or ministry to others represents a far higher level of commitment when it springs from a selfless love of God and love of our neighbor. When it comes to stewardship in ministry, virtue is not *its own reward.* It goes beyond that rationale because it is based on the scriptural idea of love. Mother Teresa epitomized the purest reason for service to others when one day, as she was washing the wounds of a street derelict, a friend commented, "I wouldn't do that for a million dollars." "Nor would I," responded the then and future saint.

Sometimes the most profound truths are expressed in simple language. I believe the most comprehensive formula for spiritual success in the stewardship of ministry was first expressed by Christ to the scribe in Matthew 22:37-39: "You must love the Lord your God with all your heart, with all your soul, and with all your mind. This is the greatest and the first commandment. The second resembles it: You must love your neighbor as yourself."

Chapter Three

MANAGING YOUR TIME ALSO MEANS MANAGING YOUR ENERGY

They that hope in the Lord will renew their strength,
They will soar as with eagles' wings,
They will run and not grow weary.

Isaiah 40:30-31

Developing, Conserving, and Spending Our Energy

The time management mania first swept the business world in the early 1970s. Although it produced many efficiencies in the workplace, it sometimes took on the facade of yet another fad. Overly enthusiastic consultants and business executives claimed that the workers who most effectively used their time would generally be among the most productive and successful. "Maximize your time and you will maximize your profits," became the rallying cry. But more seasoned business heads prevailed. They reasoned that true success in any endeavor required using a balanced set of skills and application over time, not quick fix-it solutions.

I once had a professional trainer on my staff who became the in-house expert on time management. He soon, however, became the butt of ridicule as he boasted how he constantly carried three time-schedule books around with him. His colleagues avoided him because he drove them bonkers with his constant time-management preaching. Although Bruce's[1] performance was adequate, he lacked a balanced approach to work and was never promoted. For Bruce, the means became the end. He proved to be a classic case of time management gone awry. Unfortunately, despite my sending Bruce to various management-training courses and providing him with attitude counseling, he never was able to adopt a more deliberative and balanced management style. He was either incapable or unwilling to make the necessary changes and, regrettably, never reached his full maximum potential.

In recent years behavioral scientists have emphasized the need for a balanced approach to work projects. They are of the opinion that one's ability to develop and maintain physical and psychic energy is just as important as being able to manage one's time. The president of a consulting firm recently telephoned me to explain that he was firing a gentleman whom I had recommended he hire a year earlier. "I just had to let him go, John. He had no staying power, just seemed to run out of steam before he could finish a project. Otherwise he was a good man, but we couldn't make a profit on him," he explained. I knew Luke's[2] background and family life rather well. He had a ton of worries, lacked balance in his life, and certainly did not take care of his health. He had plenty of talent but had never learned how to pace himself and focus on the priorities. There was a happy ending in Luke's situation. I took

---

[1] Name of individual cited as an example has been changed to protect his privacy.
[2] Name of individual cited as an example has been changed to protect his privacy.

him under my wing and worked with him in more effectively managing his time and talents. Luke has excellent interpersonal relations abilities and advanced computer skills. He sought medical assistance in developing an exercise program and healthier diet. Finally, he agreed to attend our parish employment committee sessions and eventually obtained a position at an attractive salary and with greater potential for advancement. Luke was successful in matching his skill set and his career likes with a niche position in a marketplace that needed both.

God Wants You Healthy To Do His Will

We Americans often talk a good game when we claim a lifestyle that is one of balanced exercise, good nutrition, and prudent health care, but the reality is quite different. We will only use our skills effectively and manage our time well when we get serious about maintaining good health. How indeed can we adequately perform ministry if we are chronically overweight, constantly fatigued, weakened by poor nutrition, and working beyond our limitations? We deceive ourselves by insisting that we have no time for these "luxuries." We may well labor zealously for the Lord, presuming in blind faith that He will directly intervene and guarantee our emotional and physical well-being while we exhaust ourselves in His service. But by doing this we defy the laws of nature and common sense.

We further deceive ourselves by rationalizing that these unhealthy circumstances are really crosses which we will bear as sacrifices to God. That's really bad theology. We are unnecessarily creating these crosses.

Sister Mary Anne Zollman, Past President of the Leadership Conference of Women Religious, U.S.A., writes: "I have learned that it is important to do things I enjoy outside my ministry, take time with friends, time for solitude, time for walks. This helps put my ministerial life in perspective and, with such perspective, what is important is seen more clearly."

Listen to what Fr. Frank J. McNulty and the late Msgr. Philip J. Murnion advised in their pamphlet for ministers, *Keeping It All in Balance*: "Self-care and one's commitment to ministry, style of ministry, and exercise of ministry all overlap. The secret of ministerial fulfillment has to do with focus and hard work and commitment, surely, but it comes down to one's ability to keep the many responsibilities of life as a minister in balance, not letting any one squeeze out the others."

The Workaholic

We all are well acquainted with the workaholics in ministry. They seem obsessed with work for the sake of work. Ministry projects alone become a priority. They abandon just about everything else in favor of work. They disdain giving their time and attention to family, friends, and other important events in their lives. It's true that many enjoy periods of unusual achievement in their ministry, but frequently they lead an unhealthy lifestyle and often prematurely end a promising career because of poor health.

But there are always the exceptions. When we read about the saints and other extraordinary ministers, we may find it difficult to distinguish between the few who may be considered radical workaholics and the many who performed ordinary things extraordinarily well. *In medio stat virtus* (virtue stands, or lies, in the middle) was one of the rudders of wisdom that guided countless monks and religious throughout the ages on their voyage to spiritual perfection. It still should be the voice of wisdom which guides us today. There is a vast difference between the Christian who is burning with zeal to do the work of Christ and the "religious time-nut" who fanatically pursues the form and volume but not substance.

Work More at "Being" and Less at "Doing"

Even Saint Ignatius Loyola, the founder of the Society of Jesus realized, in his later years, the danger of his prior excesses of penance and mortification. In his book, *Ignatius of Loyola: The Psychology of a Saint,* author W.W. Meissner, S.J., writes: "He is now no longer a fanatical extremist with a burning desire to take the kingdom by storm. The tone of *Spiritual Exercises* is measured, prudent, holding up ideals and lofty ambitions while at the same time urging moderation. He had ruined his health and destroyed his body in his impatience and immoderate zeal for self-abnegation and severe penance; he did not want his sons (Jesuits) to make the same mistakes and render themselves less, rather than more, fit for God's work." Saint Francis of Assisi came to the same conclusion after years of severe mortifications against "brother ass," as he referred to the body.

I firmly believe that the essence of holiness is "being Christ to others." This may or may not involve "doing." To manifest Christ to others by our thoughts, words, deeds, and above all, to project His presence, is the ultimate goal of ministry, and indeed, of holiness. Fr. J. O'Neill, S.J., put it a bit differently when he wrote: "The sure sign of genuine sanctity was for one to be totally present in the here and now with the person with whom one is dealing."

The late Rev. James P. McManimon, one of the principal developers of the Permanent Diaconate in the New Jersey Diocese of Trenton, eloquently expressed this guiding principle in an address to an assembly of Deacons. You may wish to substitute yourself in this description, no matter your position in ministry.

> A Deacon should not see his worth in what he is or what he does but because of who he is. It doesn't matter that you are the only Deacon in the parish, or the smartest, or the most popular, or the pastor's confidante… nor does it matter that you are quite adept at preaching, always present at every weekend Mass… do all the Baptism preparations and visit every hospital within twenty miles of the parish. What does matter is who you are. What is your relationship with God? Are you a person of prayer? Are you and your wife a manifestation of God's love to one another, to your children, to the world? In the end these are the things that matter. These are the elements that define what you are as a Deacon.

We All Have Different Degrees of Energy

All men are created equal, except when it comes to the distribution of natural energy and talents. God in His wisdom has allocated us an equal number of hours in a day but different talents and energy capacities. We can increase our reserve of energy and strength through exercise, rest, and nutrition. We can even hone our skills to the maximum degree. But the most encouraging news is this: When it comes to developing spiritual and psychic energy there appears to be no limit to our potential. We call that energy Grace or the Power of the Holy Spirit.

Dr. Albert Einstein claimed the average person used only 5% of his potential intellectual capacity. Einstein himself is said to have used only 15% of his brainpower. I find it intriguing how anyone could calculate such percentages but perhaps these analysts are using more than 15% of their brain capacity. Fortunately, there is no limit to the supply of supernatural energy because the availability of supernatural grace is infinite. We need only ask for it with "humble boldness."

The Super Servant Syndrome

I love to read epitaphs. As a matter of fact I like to collect them. One summer I spent an afternoon in an ancient cemetery in the west of Ireland searching for the tombstones of my ancestors. I was not too successful but I did find inscriptions like, "Here lies Reverend Kilduff, He Wore Himself Out in the Service of the Lord." This was not an uncommon epitaph inscribed on the tombstones of priests, ministers, and servants of the Lord in years gone by. I do not mean in any way to disparage those valiant souls. I suspect some experienced an early demise because they were afflicted with that ministry disease known as *The Super Servant Syndrome*. Even today we still hear of men and women in ministry who suffer from this malady and are eulogized as martyrs and heroes. And perhaps they are. But think of the many more productive years they might have enjoyed had they led a more balanced lifestyle.

Today, to some extent, we can control our work environment. Our days of old age, disability, and exhaustion will come soon enough. It makes more sense if we order our lives so as to be productive in ministry as long as possible. We can then help more people in meaningful ways for a longer period of time. There is a provocative poem that expresses the impossible dream many of us might wish would become a reality.

"The Wonderful One-Hoss Shay"
(also known as: The Deacon's Masterpiece)

> Have you heard of the wonderful one-hoss shay?
> That was built in such a logical way
> It ran a hundred years to a day...
> It went to pieces all at once...
> End of the wonderful one-hoss shay.
> Oliver Wendell Holmes (1809-1894)

In his poem, Holmes goes on to draw a comparison between the human body and the perfectly constructed and well-maintained one-horse carriage which ran successfully for one hundred years. Wouldn't it be wonderful if we could maintain our bodies like that famous carriage so that they would last for a hundred years, and then wear out all at once? We could dispense with suffering and the disabilities of old age, enjoy a more productive life of ministry, and sail painlessly into eternity. Of course, this is sheer fantasy for most of us, even though a few fortunate souls do achieve this ideal.

When people in ministry suffer "burnout," they deprive their community of the benefits of their gifts and their God of His glory. It seems to me when we are "laboring unceasingly" we may be pursuing our own will and not God's will. We need to heed the advice of our mentors and spiritual directors when they caution us to "forget those false guilt feelings [and] take those necessary pit-stops to recharge body and spirit." It really

26

is absurd to feel embarrassed or to make excuses when taking time for necessary leisure. This practice is simply good time management. During these hours of relaxation the Holy Spirit may be nurturing our growth, refreshing our soul, and inspiring us with thoughts that will produce fruit a "hundredfold." Some misguided ministers will boast, "I haven't had a day off or a decent vacation in years." To which I reply, "That may be well-intentioned but it's so very sad."

I Can Do All Things — The First Great Time Management Secret

> I can do all things in Jesus Christ who strengthens me.
> Philippians 4:13

This is one of those scripture passages that some overly enthusiastic modern day evangelists magnify beyond St. Paul's original intent. They interpret it as the all-encompassing power to do just about everything the mind can conceive. In contrast, ultra-conservative Christians are reluctant to believe its truly magnificent meaning. Paul does not imply that we can do things contrary to the natural laws, unless there occur those rare interventions which we call miracles. He does mean that through the power of the Holy Spirit, we can perform, in Christ's name, deeds that through our own ability would otherwise prove extremely difficult or impossible.

And that brings us to that first astounding *secret* of time management: the power of the Holy Spirit. When we tap into that tremendous source of strength we release the grace which magnifies our efforts a hundredfold. Little wonder that the disciples of Christ, who were seemingly only average men at best, performed such magnificent deeds. Why then would the Holy Spirit respond to us any differently? We Christians, who believe in this power, this special grace, have at our very fingertips the awesome ability to do great things for the Lord when we dedicate our time and talent for His purpose.

We also enjoy a major advantage over those exclusively involved in using their energies in commercial and worldly pursuits. You will rarely, if ever, read or hear any reference to this special power in the business world. But we can utilize this unique source of power in the ministerial management process. So what are we waiting for? Government task forces are continually studying energy, food, and other natural resource crises. But I feel that the spiritual energy crisis is the most critical. Joseph Grassi, writing in the *St. Anthony Messenger* magazine several years ago stated, "The greatest energy crisis today is the failure to reach the new power and untapped sources of energy that lie within our deepest selves through prayer."

So, how do we tap into this reservoir of spiritual energy? How do we access this tremendous power, or *dynamis,* referred to by Paul? The first thing we need to do is to pray for the release of the Holy Spirit in our lives. Admittedly, we did receive the gifts of the Holy Spirit at Baptism and then at Confirmation but perhaps we are not fully aware that the Holy Spirit dwells within us and we must consciously pray that He release, or renew, His power in our lives. Catholic Charismatics, as well as Pentecostalists, advocate a more formal procedure or experience called, "Being baptized in the Spirit." They seek to experience Christ and the Holy Spirit in the same way the early Christians did. Some Catholics and other Christians may seem uncomfortable with this approach even though the Charismatic Movement has been approved by the Church. Nevertheless we

28

need to think big and pray boldly to the Holy Spirit to empower us with all the spiritual gifts as recounted by Paul in his First Letter to the Corinthians, chapters 12-14.

We pray first for the seven gifts of wisdom, understanding, knowledge, counsel, piety, fortitude, and the fear of the Lord. We follow up by asking to be empowered with what Paul calls "manifestations" which are the utterance of wisdom, the utterance of knowledge, faith, healing, miracles, prophecy, the ability to distinguish between spirits, the various kinds of tongues, and the interpretation of tongues. We may conclude with a plea for the fruits of the Spirit: charity, joy, peace, patience, kindness, goodness, generosity, gentleness, faithfulness, modesty, self-control and chastity (Galatians 5:22). In chapter 13 we describe in further detail how we can increase our spiritual energy by focusing on the Indwelling of the Holy Trinity.

The Sacred Source of Energy — the Secret of Sanctity

You Will Receive Power

> You will receive power when the Holy Spirit
> comes down on you.   Acts 1:8

In their book *You Will Receive Power,* Sr. Marie Burle, C.P.P.S., and Sr. Sharon Plankenhorn, C.P.P.S., share the source of spiritual energy and the secret of sanctity by citing the Prayer of Cardinal Mercier to the Holy Spirit:

> I am going to reveal to you a secret of sanctity and
> happiness. If every day during five minutes, you will
> keep your imagination quiet, shut your eyes to all the
> things of sense, and close your ears to all the sounds of

29

earth, so as to be able to withdraw into the sanctuary of your baptized soul, which is the temple of the Holy Spirit, speaking there to that Holy Spirit, saying:

O Holy Spirit, soul of my soul, I adore you. Enlighten, guide, strengthen and console me. Tell me what I ought to do and command me to do it. I promise to be submissive in everything you permit to happen to me, only show me what is your will.

If you do this, your life will pass happily and serenely. Consolation will abound even in the midst of troubles. Grace will be given in proportion to the trial as well as strength to bear it, bringing you to the gates of paradise full of merit.

This submission to the Holy Spirit is the secret of sanctity.

Chapter Four

MANAGE YOURSELF AND YOU WILL MANAGE YOUR TIME

If you can manage, you can manage just about anything.
Anonymous

What Is This Management Mystique?

No one literally manages his time. This is a complete misnomer. What actually happens is that we manage ourselves in relation to time. I spent several years as a Program Director at the American Management Association in New York City. Every day I would interact with hundreds of business people as they gathered in the conference rooms of the AMA building in mid-Manhattan. They came to learn the intricacies of the management mystique. The AMA invited leading management experts from the world of business, academia, and government to educate those attendees who were eager to master the secrets of operating their companies more profitably and effectively.

These business luminaries lectured on the classical management topics of Goals and Objectives Setting, Planning, Organizing, Scheduling, Motivating, Implementing and Controlling. The AMA enjoyed a worldwide reputation for always being on the cutting edge of business theory and practice. But in my tenure there I observed that there was one vital topic that was never directly discussed on a formal basis. It was the keystone that supported all the other business principles. It was implicit in the whole spectrum of management commandments. That concept is called *mental discipline* — or the will to first manage oneself. It's the desire to engage — to tackle the difficult, beginning with oneself.

It's the *conditio sine qua non* for success and, lacking it, there can be no success. My Marine Drill Instructor called it the "Spirit of the Bayonet," or the will to first discipline oneself and then engage. It therefore was a foregone conclusion that, unless the business attendees were willing to discipline themselves in applying all the traditional management techniques, they could never be totally successful in business. And they must discipline themselves in relation to the time available to them. In Thomas Huxley's words: "Perhaps the most valuable result of all education is the ability to make yourself do the thing you have to do, when it ought to be done, whether you like it or not." There is no magic in the art of management in either business or ministry. We too must be willing to apply discipline in exercising management principles and especially in relation to how we handle our time and talents. We owe only the very best to God and to those entrusted to our care.

Why Are We Reluctant to Use the Most Effective Management Methods?

Some people in ministry still believe in what I now call *the myth* of the separation of church and business. Others feel there is something unclean or even "sinful" in associating business practices with church activities. There are those, including some eminent Christian business people, who proclaim that the Church and business worlds are totally different, and few, if any, management techniques used in the arena of commerce can be successfully applied in day-to-day Church activities. However, I have seen firsthand the dramatic changes in parishes and organizations which have adopted an enlightened management philosophy.

I attended an Evangelization Conference several years ago in which speaker after speaker presented innovative methods for spreading the Good News. During intermission I asked the keynote speaker, a nationally recognized authority, why the traditional door-to-door approach could not be updated and used more effectively. He stunned me with his reply, "I know you mean well," he said, "but home visitations are the last thing we should consider when evangelizing." In Marketing 101, we learned that if the clients don't come to where the product or service is being offered then you must take the service to the customer. I firmly believe we often get so involved in theory, analyses, research, and meetings that we become mired down and miss our main mission. Marketing 101 can still be applied to Ministry. Later, a fellow attendee confided that his parish Evangelization Committee had been meeting for five years. They conducted monthly meetings, hosted countless speakers, and encouraged members to attend seminars, but they never visited a single home. "Why not?" I asked. "It's so very difficult; our members are reluctant and, besides, we've never been properly trained," he replied. Ultimately, I learned his committee disbanded. I shudder to think of the time wasted and the souls potentially lost without follow-through on home visits.

In fairness to those who doubt that management techniques can be applied to ministry, I will admit that there are management models and concepts that obviously do not lend themselves to the world of ministering to others. For example, concepts like re-engineering, return on investment, customer satisfaction, and undercutting the competition don't quite fit our ministry model. But, just because some business techniques are not relevant, there is no reason why we should disregard those methods that prove to be applicable.

The Most Rev. David A. Zubik, former Auxiliary Bishop and Vicar General for the Diocese of Pittsburgh, Pennsylvania and current Bishop of Green Bay, Wisconsin was the keynote speaker at the 2002 Convention of the NACPA (National Association of Church Personnel Administrators) in Orlando, Florida. In his address concerning the challenges facing the Church he stated:

> The first of these challenges is the role of the Church being "Church and business" at the same time. On the one hand, we are a Church. We are the Body of Christ. We are community. But at the same time, the Church is also a business and we are compelled, as Church, to be Church according to the best business practices. We need accountability for money and for employees. We need business plans for diocesan corporations, for parish committees, for religious congregations. We need to operate on profit over loss or have suitable plans to cover programs which fail to do so. Both who

we are as Church — our mission and how we operate as church–as–business are necessary components. To ignore either of these components prevents us from being who we are called as leaders.

We should be encouraged when we see more and more Christian communities applying modern management concepts in their local ministerial activities. Witness the many creative advertising campaigns now used in vocational recruiting as well as the professional appeals to woo back alienated Catholics. It is also gratifying to see the rapid growth of Lay Ecclesial programs in many dioceses and the hiring of business managers in a growing number of parishes. Stewardship programs encourage lay people to implement the same management skills which they use in their everyday jobs. Lay leadership has advanced in the Church dramatically since Vatican II. But sadly enough, some misguided members of the clergy still resist this so called "power sharing." In their book, *Executive Summary of Parishes and Parish Ministries — A Study of Parish Lay Ministry,* David DeLambo and the late Msgr. Philip J. Murnion state, "Parishes are becoming more 'intentional,' i.e., producing more mission statements, engaging in more planning, and regularly using pastoral councils in eighty-eight percent of the parishes, and finance councils in ninety-three percent."

Over the years I have conducted hundreds of parish Capital Fundraising Campaigns as well as Stewardship Programs. I had ample opportunity to carefully listen to parishioners as they expressed their opinions and concerns about ministry. Listen to some of their typical suggestions in relation to ministry:

> We want our priests to be free to pastor and minister to our spiritual needs; hire professional managers to handle the business administration; Father was never trained to run the business aspects of a parish; let the

35

laity do the finance, budgeting, and accounting jobs since they are better equipped for these roles.

In recent years there has been much positive response to these parishioner pleas. What was once considered theory is now becoming reality. The declining availability of priests coupled with the willingness of competent laity to become more involved is changing the profile of parishes into models of truly shared ministry.

Chapter Five

SETTING YOUR GOALS FOR MINISTRY

This one thing I do,
forgetting those things which are behind
And reaching forth unto those things which are before,
I press to the goal for the prize
of the high calling of God in Christ.

Philippians 3:13-14

Paul, the Penultimate Goal Setter

It surely sounds to me like St. Paul, in the above passage, was talking about pursuing a goal. In his travels he must have observed the various Roman games. He probably borrowed from the vocabulary of the athletes when he used the word *epekteinomenos* (easier to perform than to pronounce), which means, *pressing, reaching, grasping for a goal.* The athlete was racing to win, to achieve his goal, and would tolerate no distraction. Paul would have us do likewise, by setting spiritual goals, never looking back, and pressing on for the eternal prize.

The 1953 Yale graduating class was asked to write down the career goals which they desired to achieve once they left the

37

University. Only 3% complied by writing their goals. When interviewed, twenty years later, it was determined that those 3% had achieved more in terms of honor, prestige, and success than the combined results realized by the 97% non-goal graduates. Incredible? I thought so. That presents a pretty powerful proof for the wisdom of setting goals. Isn't it astounding that the majority of those supposedly very intelligent students from such a prestigious institute of learning could not visualize the benefit of mapping the course of their future careers?

Management by Objectives Becomes Ministry by Objectives

I remember attending management seminars many years ago conducted by a very impressive consultant named Peter Drucker. In 1954, he developed the process called *"Management by Objectives,"* better known as MBO in the business circles of that day. It is called by various names in the current business texts but the principles remain the same. The concept revolutionized the way many American companies did business. Many business owners thought productivity meant making their workers conduct multiple activities and to be "busy at being busy." *Management by Objectives* changed much of that. Business owners were now substituting specific goals in lieu of multiple procedures and regulations.

I will take Drucker's definition of MBO and simply adapt it to the concept of ministry. Here it is: "MBO is a process whereby the superior (*God, Bishop, Pastor, Board of Directors*) and the subordinates (*you and I*) of an organization (*church, committee, community*) jointly identify its common goals, define each individual's area of responsibility in terms of results expected, and then use these measures for operating the unit (*church, committee, community*) and assess the respective contributions of each of the members." Now that's a fairly long-winded way of saying, "Managing by objectives for results." Managing by Objectives, or its contemporary equivalent, has been integrated into the overall management process by most of Fortune's 500. True, it has taken on many refinements over the years, but the theory and practice are sound. They work. It helps businesses become productive and profitable. I feel that we who wish to become "profitable servants" for the Lord should consider adopting these techniques. In our vineyard of activity, MBO should be translated to *Ministry by Objectives.* I am confident as we continue to explore new and better ways to spread the Gospel we will in some ways be forced to use only the most efficient methodologies available. God and His message are worthy of only the best.

Why Should We Set Spiritual/Ministry Goals?

Most of us are required to establish goals and objectives in our job, profession, or chosen career. Why then not set goals for our ministry? We are, after all, working for the ultimate CEO and for our eternal reward.

Here are some reasons for setting spiritual goals:

• *To Become More Effective and Efficient*

Effectiveness means we will do the right thing in ministry and in the correct manner. A well thought-out ministry goal insures that we have selected the most meaningful mission.

39

- *To Focus On the Most Important and Not the Trivial*

Our goals will force us to concentrate our time and expertise on the critical as well as the important; they will help us avoid the "activity trap."

- *To Maximize Our Efforts*

We will multiply the effect by reaching a larger audience in a more intensive manner. It's called "getting more bang for the buck."

- *To Divert Daydreams and Distractions*

We can remove fuzzy thinking and emotional flights of fancy that frequently tend to obscure our major objective. We can also avoid skipping from one project to another.

- *To Establish Benchmarks for Measuring Results*

"How am I doing?" was New York City's Mayor Koch's favorite question to his constituents. We all want feedback on how well we are progressing. Goals give us standards or a base line against which we can evaluate our relative success or failure.

- *To Enjoy Peace of Mind*

When we are pursuing the best possible program compared to all the possible alternatives we will derive a tremendous sense of satisfaction.

- *To Receive a Confidence Boost*

Periodic monitoring of our goals and their related activities will encourage us to continue with enthusiasm.

40

Why Are We Reluctant to Set Spiritual/Ministry Goals?

We fail to establish goals for ministry for many of the same reasons we are reluctant to set them in our jobs or other areas of our lives.

Listen to the following reasons and excuses we frequently use with regard to goal-setting in ministry:

• *Goals Are Incompatible With Matters of the Spirit*

By some curious quirk of logic we may reason that goals simply don't lend themselves to things spiritual since only God can and should measure our progress.

• *We Never Considered It*

It never crossed our minds nor have we ever heard of such a bizarre idea.

• *Fear of Failure*

Guilt is bad enough, so why add the possibility of embarrassment should we fail to meet self-imposed goals.

• *Laziness*

It's just too much of a bother; besides, no one in the Bible ever did it.

• *Procrastination*

It's a wonderful idea; perhaps I'll get around to it tomorrow.

41

- *Too Difficult and Complex*

I really don't know how. It seems like a lot of work. I'm not sure it's worth it.

Now that we have put most of the objections to spiritual goal-setting out in the open and also reviewed some of the benefits, let's look at how to use the process.

How to Set Ministry Goals

> May you attain full knowledge of God's will
> through perfect wisdom and spiritual insight.
> Colossians 1:9

- *First We Must Find Out What "The Boss" Wants*

I worked for several large corporations and also was involved in running several small businesses. Invariably, when that time of year arrived for setting budgets it also meant it was time to define our goals for the coming year. Frankly, I often found the budgeting and goal-setting process to be among the more difficult parts of my job, probably because profitability and sometimes survival depended so much on making the right choices and predictions. The process actually became the road map which determined whether we succeeded or failed. The first thing I did was meet with my boss or partner — everyone has one or more, even Presidents and Popes. Unless I knew what my superior considered the priority objectives for the corporation, I realized I would soon be in trouble. Sure, I could come up with the most ambitious goals and possibly achieve some of them, but I still would have failed if they were not what the boss or President wanted. It had to be a joint venture. I needed to work closely with my partner, boss, or a team

42

member if I wanted to help them achieve the company's goals and keep my job.

I feel that we need to use a similar approach in ministry by setting mutual goals. Well, how do we really know what "The Boss" wants when it comes to formulating our spiritual goals? Fortunately, there are several steps we can take to get the answers.

• *Schedule an Appointment with God*

That's right, just tell God you would like to set up a visit with Him to discuss some of the most important ventures you would like to undertake in your ministry, subject of course to His Will and Divine Plan. I recently asked the Reverend Damien Thompson, the Abbot of the Abbey of Gethsemani in Trappist, Kentucky, how he sets his goals. He replied, "The Lord sets the goals for me. I just perform them as they present themselves." Admittedly, the members of the Cistercian Order of Strict Observance live and minister in an environment much different than most of us. But, the Abbot went directly to the "Top" for his goal guidance, and we also need to first go directly to God despite our different lifestyles.

Sr. Mary Zollman, B.V.M, Past President of Leadership Conference of Women Religious, U.S.A., approaches it in a similar manner. She wrote:

> The first and most important thing I do is spend significant quiet time each morning with God. I consciously bring to mind people, the meetings, and the events of that particular day and intentionally take time to breathe God into each one. Then, I breathe out that life of God, praying as I do, that I will be that presence of God in the lives of those people and in those daily

43

events and activities. This morning time calms my whole being and helps me be aware that what matters is not the amount of things I accomplish but the quality of love I bring to each person and task.

• *Collaborate with Community or Parish Ministry*

Frequently our personal spiritual goals will intermesh with the needs and goals of our community, parish, or people in other ministries. We need to make sure that our personal spiritual goals do not present a major conflict with the common spiritual goals of the community. Fr. Thomas Krosnicki, S.V.D., Provincial of the Society of the Divine Word, writes, "My goals are generated by my Council and by the needs that arise." Deacon William Ditewig, Executive Director Secretariat for Diaconate, suggests the following as a good format in determining goals: "Pope John Paul II's Apostolic Exhortation *Pastores Dabo Vobis* identifies four dimensions for Priestly, Diaconal and Lay Ministry formation: the human, the spiritual, the intellectual, and the pastoral." Ditewig further comments, "It can serve as a framework for setting our goals for our own human development, spiritual life, academic and ministerial preparation as well as pastoral skills. Using this approach helps us to avoid getting trapped into one or the other, and neglecting the rest."

Sr. Zollman explains the collaborative approach in a little different way. She writes, "I purposely work with a team and engage, around a particular project, those persons most immediately involved in the dynamic of that project. I never feel or work as though the project is my own." And further, "Goals are uncovered by being sensitive to the members, and the members carry those directions forward with some facilitation by us as leaders. Rather than leadership setting goals, we focus or channel the energies of the membership."

- *Pray the "Perfect Prayer"*

We begin with a prayer for guidance and wisdom from the Holy Spirit. You probably have your favorite prayer. Mine is a twelve-word summary from several powerful verses in St. Paul's Letter to the Colossians 1:9-12. This is my synopsis: *"Lord, help me to know your will and give me the strength to do it."* I call it my perfect prayer because it seems to say it all. How can we go wrong if we are doing the will of God? And if He wants us to do His will He has to give us the necessary strength to perform it. Just knowing we are doing God's will bring us a certain serenity of soul. St. Thomas Aquinas wrote: "A man's heart is light when he wills what God wills." Matthew Kelly, in his book *The Rhythm of Life,* writes: "In my life I believe that everything good comes from knowing and living the will of God."

During our formal appointment with God we use prayer, scripture, and meditation. Then we need to listen as well as speak if we are to completely discern His will. I am always impressed when I hear how some of the biblical characters, the saints, and even contemporary souls, have actually spoken to God directly, or claim to have had the experience of hearing His voice. But the rest of us will have to settle for indirect communication — which probably is just as effective for most of us.

- *Be Completely Open to God's Plan*

As much as I enjoy Frank Sinatra's legendary crooning voice and lyrics, there remains one song whose words would run counter to the point I wish to make. Remember his popular song, "I Did It My Way"? Its message represents the independent, aggressive attitude that has come to typify the macho

American male. In some situations in life, especially when one's survival may be at risk, such an attitude may be justified. When it comes to discerning and doing God's will however, we need to adopt a completely opposite approach. Perhaps we should be saying to God, "I will no longer do it my way but your way, O Lord." The lyrics "Show me the Way Lord That I Have to Go," taken from "One Day At A Time," by Marijohn Wilkin and Kris Kristofferson, might be more appropriate when seeking to follow God's direction for us.

• *Contemplate: "What Do I Want From God?"*

Your answer to this question will tell you a lot about yourself. Some typical responses include: "Please grant me and my loved ones good health, happiness, security, a good job, friends, freedom from all harm, etc." We seem to engage in a lifetime debating match with God. On the one hand we desire and pray for so many good things to happen to us, and on the other hand we may sincerely attempt to turn everything over to Divine Providence. The saints and those well on the way towards perfection simply abandon themselves totally to God's will.

• *Contemplate: "What Does God Want From Me?"*

The answers abound in Scripture:

> I have called you by name and you are mine.
>
> Isaiah 43:1
>
> It was not you who chose me, but I who chose you and appointed you to go and bear fruit that will remain, go therefore and make disciples of all nations.
>
> John 15:8
>
> Come follow me. I am the Way, the Truth, and the Life.
>
> John 14:6

46

Be forewarned. God respects our freedom to cooperate with His grace. But once we start the process of setting our goals for God, we should be prepared to listen to the voice of the Holy Spirit. It may sound soft and almost silent but it is relentless. That "quiet violence" of the Holy Spirit will revisit us again and again if we are willing to be silent and receptive.

- *Consult a Spiritual Director, Confessor, Pastor or Trusted Mentor*

The next step in discerning our spiritual goals is to discuss them with a spiritual director, if we are fortunate enough to have one, or a pastor, confessor, or a mature and trusted friend. The ancient Celtic mystics often wrote about the need for an *"Anam Cara,"* or soul friend, if one is to make spiritual progress. We all need some type of spiritual confidante or soul friend.

When we openly discuss our goals with these counselors we are really opening ourselves up to the Holy Spirit. They can give us invaluable advice, sound direction, and a reality check. They can protect us from delusions and those ill-advised ventures that afflict both the novice and the veteran in ministry.

- *Write Your Goals, or Risk Possible Failure*

> Now come, write it on a tablet they can keep,
> inscribe it in a record that it may in future days
> be an eternal witness.   Isaiah 30:8

We have now thought about, prayed over, and discussed our potential goals with all those who should be involved in the process. This is an excellent beginning but we can't just stop there. Experts tell us that unless we actually write down our goals there is a good chance we will never achieve them. Remember the example of the Yale students? Fifteen-hundred years ago, St. Benedict, in his wisdom, stipulated as his first rule that monks in making their solemn profession of vows of stability, obedience, and conversion of life (which includes poverty and chastity), must write down on parchment their sacred promises and then place them on the altar as a sign of their total commitment. The very act of putting vows, goals, or promises in writing produces a profound sense of responsibility that immeasurably transcends the symbolic act of merely putting pen to paper.

You can also reinforce your potential for success by sharing your resolutions with a few select confidantes. Sincere friends will motivate you to succeed by encouraging you and exerting subtle peer pressure.

You will find Exhibit 1, *My Goals for God and Strategies to Achieve Them* in the Appendix at the end of this book. This exhibit should make the goal-setting practice much easier. I must confess that when I am requested to complete a form, quiz, or exhibit in a text which may be similar to this one, I will often just continue reading. I may fill in a few answers and vow to return to the exhibit later, but continue reading the rest of the text. I therefore understand if you also are tempted to do this, but urge you to periodically refer to these exhibits to help you understand the whole procedure. You should consider recording the answers in a journal rather than in this book, which you might want to pass along.

You may wish to start with your Three-Month Goals. You can then gradually work up to your One-Year Goals and eventually your Lifetime Goals. Remember to apply the SAM test: the goal must be Specific, Achievable, and Measurable.

Here are some examples of goals and their related strategies or activities:

GOAL: To Have Established A Scripture Study Program by June 1.

STRATEGIES:
1. Survey parishioners to determine the need for, and interest in, a Bible Study Program.
2. Determine which of the commercially available study programs best suit the parishioners' needs.
3. Recruit and train a qualified facilitator.
4. Secure a suitable meeting location.
5. Conduct a publicity program.
6. Develop a budget, schedule, and matrix checklist.

GOAL: To Have Organized an Evangelization Visitation Project for 10% of the Community by September 15.

STRATEGIES:
1. Recruit and train twenty volunteer visitors.
2. Identify the target population to be visited.
3. Communicate program to church members.
4. Develop a budget, schedule, and media procedure.
5. Design a feedback and evaluation process.

GOAL: To Have Achieved a Masters Degree in Pastoral Ministry by May 1.

STRATEGIES:
1. Seek spiritual guidance on the soundness of this project.
2. Survey colleges and universities that best accommodate my situation concerning travel, tuition, schedule, and expenses.
3. Secure support and approval from potential employers and those who may need my services.

4. Develop a schedule compatible with my family, job, and social obligations.
5. Design a realistic study schedule that will assist me in doing quality work and achieving passing grades.

One of the most common mistakes we can make in defining goals is to confuse them with the strategies or activities we must engage in to achieve the goal. You cannot "do" a goal, but you can do an activity or perform a number of strategies which will eventually help you accomplish your goal. Activities and strategies are the means or steps one does in order to finally reach the goal. It may make it clearer if you remember your goal is the end product or final culmination of dozens, or even hundreds, of enabling activities you must perform to achieve your goal.

Why not try entering on Exhibit 1, or in a Journal, your own three-month goals with the necessary activities to achieve them? At a later time, perhaps while you are on a retreat or during a special quiet time, you can complete your One-Year and Lifetime Goals. With practice, you will soon discover the ease with which you can convert what were formerly only mental goals to specific, meaningful commitments on paper, and finally to action. But much more important for you will be the satisfaction you will experience in taking this giant step.

A Sobering Scenario — Your Individual Life Span

Let's assume you just visited your doctor for an annual checkup. He detects some disturbing symptoms and orders further diagnostic tests. Upon your return to his office he soberly gives you the news that so many dread to hear, "I'm sorry, Bill, but the tests reveal you have cancer." "How much time do I have Doc?" you mutter. He looks at you and whispers, "Only God knows for sure, but in your case I would estimate about three or four months." Now that you have recovered somewhat from the shock, I have a question for you: "HOW WILL YOU SPEND THOSE FINAL THREE MONTHS OF YOUR LIFE?" To simplify the situation let us assume that all your medical, funeral, and household bills, as well as general debts, have been paid. Just take your pen and pad and write down all those things that now are the most important for you to do in this short period of time you have left. When I once posed this question at a seminar, one elderly lady raised her hand and jokingly announced, "The first thing I would do would be to seek a second opinion." Of course, the point of this exercise is to be taken seriously. It's important that you write down the priority things you want to do or accomplish, and then share them with your spouse, family, and friends.

I will now pose two further questions. The first: "IF YOU IDENTIFIED THOSE THINGS THAT WERE THE MOST IMPORTANT IN YOUR LIFE TO DO, WHY AREN'T YOU DOING THEM NOW?" Think about that for a moment. The sudden shock that you had only ninety days of your life remaining immediately made you focus on the people and things in your life that really mattered. Well, why aren't you doing the most important things now? I've heard all the reasons and excuses. This leads me to the second question: "WHAT GUARANTEE IS THERE THAT YOU HAVE 30, 60, OR 90 DAYS, OR EVEN TOMORROW?" So I must ask the question of you again, "Why don't you start now? If you don't, how can you be sure you ever will?"

Refer to your list during your daily meditation and prayers. Incorporate it into your spiritual goal setting program. But do something about it now. Listen to Christ's exhortation concerning the uncertainty of our time span: "But God said to him, 'You fool, this very night your life will be demanded of you'" (Luke 12:20) and, again, "You must also be prepared, for at an hour you do not expect, the Son of Man will come" (Luke 12:40).

Actuarial Statistics

For seventeen years I was employed by a large insurance company that made billions in profits by predicting how many people would die at a certain age, how many would become sick and disabled, and the dollar costs that would be incurred. The company employed dozens of actuaries who calculated these figures, and their projections were correct most of the time. That's how life insurance companies make most of their money. One day I asked Sam, an actuary friend of mine, how long I had to live according to his actuarial tables. At that time I had reached the ripe old age of fifty. "Well" replied Sam, "it involves many variables, but in your case I would estimate that you could live to age 72." I might have dismissed Sam's prediction by invoking my mother-in-law's favorite expression, "God spoke before us all." Instead, I interpreted his response as another "moment of grace" and renewed my resolve to maximize my use of every hour and day the Lord would still give me. Incidentally, as I write this book, I have exceeded Sam's mortality prediction by three years — thanks be to God.

You might wish to consider a similar assessment of your own mortality. I'll make it easy for you to quickly calculate your actuarial life expectancy. I would ask the female readers to jot down the figure 84 and then deduct their current age from that figure. (I promise you I won't look). Gentlemen readers should write the figure 72, and then subtract their current age. The difference, anxious readers, between these two figures will represent the estimated years you have yet to live. Some of you may have already outlived these statistical tables, so congratulations are in order. Even though these figures are only general estimates, most of us will be shocked, or a bit surprised. I hope this serves as a gentle reminder of the brevity of our lives and the opportunity still remaining for us to make significant changes.

I am reluctant to leave this chapter without giving you one more suggestion for extending your life span or improving the quality of your remaining years. Several years ago a life insurance company in West Germany discovered in a study that husbands who kissed their wives before leaving for work in the morning lived five years longer than the males who did not. They also earned 20% more in salary and experienced less sickness and disability. Obviously the kissing habit was simply an indicator of a well-balanced individual who probably did other things in his life that were conducive to good health. So here is an opportunity for you to actuarially extend your life through a pleasant habit. The study incidentally projects similar benefits for the spouses. If you do not have a spouse, take courage, since there exists another study stating those who have a pet dog or cat are significantly healthier and may live longer. A hug and a kiss seem to produce more benefits than we realize. Another study suggests we need to give and get at least a hundred hugs a day — are you getting your share?

> You have no idea what your life will be like tomorrow.
> You are a puff of smoke that briefly appears
> and then disappears. James 4:14

Chapter Six

PLANNING TO ACHIEVE YOUR GOALS

For I know well the plans I have in mind for you,
    says the Lord,
Plans for your welfare not for evil;
plans to give you a future full of hope.
                                    Jeremiah 29:11

A goal without a plan is just a wish.
                        Antoine de Saint Exupery (1900-1944)

When we make New Year's resolutions we rarely back them up with a detailed plan. That is one of the reasons why we fail to keep those good resolutions. And we all know how the road to hell is paved. High hopes and good intentions are poor substitutes for a plan. We need to wrap muscle and sinew around our skeletal goals.

In the prior chapter, we discussed how to set goals and identify the strategies to achieve them. Now we need to incorporate our goals into an overall realistic plan of action. Planning is simply mentally bringing the future into the present so we can do something about it now. That's why we conduct rehearsals for plays and weddings. Planning may also be defined as making a mental picture of a future accomplishment.

55

Visualization and Imaging: The Mission

> Your sons and daughters shall prophesy,
> your old men shall dream dreams,
> Your young men shall see visions.
>
> Joel 3:1

I was among the smallest guys in my class in Grammar and High School. It should prove no surprise when I reveal that I experienced more than my share of school yard fighting. Lack of size always poses some challenges. When I failed to make the school baseball team I settled for a position on the softball team. I could handle some field positions but failed miserably at bat. One afternoon the opposing pitcher made the mistake of delivering the ball in just the right plane in which I was swinging my bat. To this day I can still feel the solid thump of wood against ball, and the surprised look in the eyes of the expert shortstop, Gene Miller, when my line drive cut through his upraised glove and sailed into the outfield and then under a stand of pine trees. When I reached home plate, I heard our German professor, standing nearby, remark, "Wow, that little guy can really smack the ball." His comment ignited a conviction in me that I could do just about anything in life if I really focused on it.

Hearing that comment made my spirits soar. I can't adequately describe that sweet sensation of achievement in hitting that home run, the cheers of my teammates, and the realization I could finally do it. That night I slept very little. I replayed the scene over and over in my mind, relishing every detail. The next day, after classes, I confidently strode to the plate armed with my newfound formula — and promptly struck out. But I wasn't discouraged. I knew I must "act as if" I would hit another home run. I would visualize the same motions that worked the day before. My next several attempts produced some great hits. I was so excited about discovering this fantastic "secret." Years later I learned my act of envisioning was no secret after all. It had been common knowledge in most cultures for many centuries. Since that day's discovery I have successfully used my "secret" in many situations throughout my life. Professional sports teams, the military, actors, and others have been using it for years. Some professional basketball teams spend as much as one-third of their practice sessions shooting imaginary baskets over and over in their minds. Much has been written about this mind game or visualization phenomenon. It has been validated, and it works. Some people prefer to call it *"perfection dreaming"* or *"envisioning."* It's all the same concept, which means we picture in our mind's eye with as much detail and as frequently as possible how we already are achieving our desired goal.

Modern motivational speakers are fond of proclaiming this famous saying, "What the mind can conceive the will can achieve." But Virgil, the Roman poet, first wrote it back in 67 B.C. saying, "They can do all because they think they can." Henry Ford put it a little differently, "If you think you can, or think you can't, you're right." That great dynamic motivational preacher and writer Norman Vincent Peale, in his book *Imaging – The Powerful Way to Change Your Life,* writes:

> There is a powerful and mysterious force in human nature that is capable of bringing dramatic improvement in our lives. It is a kind of mental engineering that works best when supported by a strong religious faith. That word is *imaging,* derived from imagination. Imaging is positive thinking carried one step further. In imaging, one does not merely think about a hoped-for goal; one "sees" or visualizes it with tremendous intensity, reinforced by prayer.

Proper planning involves our "seeing" the big picture of our goal or ministry first, then organizing the necessary activities that will help us attain the identified goal. Some of us plan in a haphazard manner. We flounder and flail away in a flurry of mindless activities, but sadly we are really going nowhere. We equate speed and motions with planning. Perhaps we are like the airline pilot who was lost in a torrential storm and then radioed the airport control tower, "Yes sir, I agree I'm probably lost but I'm sure making great time."

We have to admire those disciplined people who, before taking on a project, will sit down and think through the whole process. Then they write out their plan of action. Usually they are extremely busy people but they have mastered the art of visualization. We can too. "If you want a job done give it to a busy person," is a business byword. What this really means is that you should give it to an organized person, one who takes time to plan, to visualize, and then act decisively.

Picking Priorities

> There's a time for some things, a time for all things,
> a time for great things, and a time for small things.
> Miguel de Cervantes (1547-1616)

I once worked for a boss who was a lawyer's lawyer. He was gifted with a logical mind and a disciplined character. He taught me the ABC's of planning my priorities. He made sure that my goals and priorities closely reflected his own. Once we agreed on my goals and strategies, Bob would ask me to divide my daily tasks or activities into three categories and label them 'A–must do'; 'B–very helpful to do'; 'C–nice to do.' "If at the end of the day," he advised, "you have only completed the 'A' priorities, I will be very satisfied. If you also complete all or most of the 'B' priorities I will be satisfied but a bit surprised. And if you complete all the 'C' priorities I will be disappointed since I will assume you spent too little time on your 'A' and 'B' priorities. Most days I had difficulty just completing my 'A' priorities. At the end of the month I had an entire file filled with 'C' tasks and a few 'B' priorities. But the salary increases and the promotions still came through. You can probably understand why. To this day I will try to determine from my many bosses just what they consider to be the ABC's in the hierarchy of priorities. By now you may be thinking that when it comes to ministry one can't analyze, divide, and categorize activity priorities. "After all," you might reason, "ministry is not like a business." But I submit it is very much like conducting a business — the business of God.

In response to my recent survey, Fr. Joseph Champlin wrote the following about priorities: "Establishing goals flows out of what are the *Priorities* in my life." He then refers to the document, *New Parish Ministries*, published by the National Pastoral Center, as serving as a basis for establishing his pastoral priorities. In that study, commissioned by the American Bishops, the authors found that dynamic parishes have these common ingredients: good Sunday worship and preaching; a practical bent to the activities of the parish; shared decision making and possibilities for active development on many levels.

A Sloppy Desk Is the Sign of a Sloppy Mind

The second lesson I learned from my boss Bob came with some humorous overtones. He would enter my office, glance at my cluttered desk, and mutter, "When did the hurricane hit?"

People are divided into two groups when it comes to arranging their offices, living quarters, and possessions. Some are "*neatniks,*" while others might be called "*slobniks.*" I belonged to the latter group, rather sloppy when it came to arranging my files, papers, books, and equipment. Bob was a "*neatnik.*" He never had more than one file or piece of paper on his desk at one time. He made it a point to focus on one task at a time. My desk, in contrast, was a very busy place. I protested that I always knew where everything was despite the apparent chaos. Of course this was not always true. One day Bob presented me with a plaque that read, "A Sloppy Desk Is the Sign of a Sloppy Mind." I soon found another plaque and sneaked it onto his desk. It had the following inscription, "If a Sloppy Desk Is the Sign of a Sloppy Mind, Then What Is an Empty Desk the Sign of?" I don't remember his reaction but I did learn to arrange my materials and activities so that I could focus on the most important things and not worry about those tasks of lesser value.

Here are some hints that may help you.

- Identify the necessary activities related to your goal and then prioritize them to effectively achieve that goal.
- Rank-order your activities the same way you ranked your goals.
- Prioritize your activities to force yourself to separate the important from the trivial and less important.
- Weigh the relative importance of each activity, then reconcile and resolve apparent conflicts.

The Art of the Trade-Off or the Sensible Solution

The raw reality is that we can never do all there is to do or all we want to do. The number of all possible ministry activities we may be called upon to do can be overwhelming. People drawn to ministry typically want to please everybody.

I hear this constant complaint, "I just can't say NO." But of course you can, and must, if you wish to ultimately be effective and save your sanity. Planning by priority simply helps us to trade off or give up doing activities of lesser importance for those of greater value. This advice may sound simplistic, but it is vital if we want to intelligently manage the bewildering number of people, projects, and programs forever competing for our precious resource — our time. Our goal is the ultimate destination, while our activities represent the journey.

Reverend Joseph Champlin contributes this bit of wisdom: "In pastoral ministry, it's also imperative to recognize that we will not be able to get all things done that we would like to do. Consequently, we must deal with the ambiguity of work not done or accomplished that we would like to do, even though there is time enough to accomplish what God wants us to do."

Chapter Seven

ORGANIZING YOUR LIFE TO ACHIEVE YOUR GOALS

Recognize Where You Are Before You Change Direction

If you don't know where you are going,
you may wind up someplace else.

Yogi Berra

The following story is so ancient it has whiskers. The balloonist was caught in a storm and was forced to make a sudden landing in a field. He caught sight of a man reading a Bible and shouted, "Sir, perhaps you can help me. You see, the hangar manager miscalculated badly and that's why I'm in this embarrassing predicament. He gave me poor directions and defective equipment. Can you tell me exactly where I am?" "Certainly," replied the man in black. "You landed in farmer Finnegan's cornfield adjacent to Route 33." "You must be a minister," responded the balloonist. "Well, yes I am, but how did you know that?" "Because the information you gave me is probably correct, but absolutely useless." "And you, young man" smiled the Minister, "are apparently a Deacon." "You're correct, but how could you possibly know that?" retorted the surprised balloonist. "Very easily," said the Minister. "You are lost, you don't know where you are headed, you didn't plan your trip very well, and now you are blaming everyone for your predicament."

If we don't know where we are going in life we may be doomed to wander aimlessly through the years and end up frustrated and disillusioned. You have probably met them — they usually are the men and women in their forties and fifties who are still trying to "find themselves," and their proper niche in life. This is especially sad for those in ministry. They may have the noblest of intentions but have no clear or consistent direction in their lives. And so they wander from one ministry to another, from one movement to the next popular program, and then wonder why their lives are so ineffective. They become lost but can blame none but themselves. Thus far we have attempted to set our goals in ministry and to identify the necessary steps to achieve them. We have also established an overall plan or vision of our mission. Now it's time to begin organizing the daily activities which really represent the nuts and bolts of our master plan.

Logging Your Life

Few of us can accurately identify with precision how we really spend our time. Think of the last project you completed and compare the time it actually took you to do it with the estimated number of hours you figured the job would take. The difference in time can be surprising, even painful. Most of us are not that good at estimating time requirements unless we are consultants or engineers. Even the experts are notorious for underestimating the actual time required to perform a function. Most people overestimate their energy reserves and ability to perform tasks within a limited time frame. I ask the following question at every time management seminar which I conduct, "What is the most effective mechanism we can use to document how we will spend the next twenty-four hours?" Rarely do I receive the answer I'm seeking. One fail-proof process would be to hire a person, preferably a stranger, to videotape your every waking hour for the next few days. This approach, however, might prove impractical or even downright embarrassing.

The Time Log of Your Life — What You See Is Where You Are

The next best method for monitoring our lives, unpopular as it is, still remains the tool of choice by most time management consultants. It's that much-maligned process we call the "Time Log." You may find it a bit tedious to complete but it will produce remarkably revealing results. The Time Log will help you quickly identify how you and others waste your time and your life. You will be both surprised and discouraged. Use it conscientiously for several weeks and eventually you will find the answers to those questions you keep asking yourself:

How can I determine where my time goes?

Life is passing me by; what can I do to control it?

I'm trapped on this merry-go-round of activities; how can I find time to do what I need and want to do?

How can I find time for God, prayer, and ministry when I have all those demands on me?

You may wish to refer to Exhibit 2, *My Time Log* in the Appendix at the end of this book. I suggest you select several days a week, for three weeks, to complete this Log. It may seem like a waste of time and even a boring exercise, but in the end you will have a realistic picture of how you are spending those precious hours of your life. While this Time Log applies to persons in all walks of life, the headings selected by ministers should represent ministerial activities.

How We Spend Our Lives

According to John R. Robinson's book, *How Americans Spend Time*, the average American spends 80% or 133 hours of the 168 hours in a week in the so-called obligatory activities. He spends 20% or 35 hours a week in discretionary or free-time functions. Looking at it in another way we spend 20 years sleeping, 5 years dressing, 6 years staring at the television, 3 years waiting, 1 year telephoning (add 50% if you use a cell phone), and 3 months tying your shoes (those discalced monks have the right idea). If you are surprised at these statistics, then consider how much time the average American spends in his lifetime just waiting for traffic signals — it's an astonishing six months. Just think of all the positive things we could be accomplishing during those moments, instead of fretting and frittering them away.

Defeating Our Time Wasters

We may create our own time-wasters, or have them imposed on us by other people or events. I have discovered that when I ask people to identify the various events or factors which waste their time, they typically identify less than a dozen. That's why we call those culprits "time thieves." We are often unaware

66

how insidiously they operate in relieving us of those precious jewels of our time. Admittedly, some interruptions are beyond our control, but with proper planning and discipline we can control or reduce many of them. For example, when you schedule an appointment you can set the parameters by suggesting the duration, objectives, date, place, and time. You can also request that the client call you to confirm his attendance. This can go a long way in reducing the irritation of the "no show."

When asked at a Time Management seminar to identify his time wasters, a young man inquired, "Do I have to give the real names of my friends and associates?" He was on the right track since many of our friends, associates, and fellow employees do waste a significant amount of our time — we let them. But the major part of the blame lies at our own door. Take a look at Exhibit 3, *Typical Time Wasters*, in the Appendix at the end of this book.

You will notice, from the Exhibit, that the number of typical time-wasters which we impose on ourselves exceeds those which are caused by others. Since we are usually the main culprits, we have the power to eliminate or at least control many of these "thieves of time." My most irritating nemesis is #6 on the first list: Can't say "No." I have wrestled with this problem for years. One colleague says I probably never learned that there really is an "N" and an "O" in the alphabet. In my defense it can be said that when one is involved in ministry, it is not as easy to turn someone away or refuse service as it is in a pure business situation. Perhaps a compromise is in order. I try handling these quandaries by gently suggesting the reasons for my inability to give assistance. I then try to soften the blow by giving some advice as the case warrants.

You may want to review the Time-Waster lists again, select those that point the finger of suspicion at you, and resolve to work on just a few each day. You will soon discover how creative you will become in discouraging those "thieves" who come knocking on your door each day.

Making Your Daily "To-Do" List for God

That brings us to discussing a major tool or mechanism that most successful people use very effectively. They employ it as a vehicle to translate their goals into reality. It's called the DAILY TO-DO LIST. Take a look at Exhibit 4, the *Daily To-Do List For God*, which is located in the Appendix at the end of this book. You may wish to modify it by incorporating your business and social activities into this list or by designing your own. Your spiritual activities should relate to your spiritual goals, if possible. Remember, activities are the steps or strategies you do in order to achieve your goals.

When I was in full-time employment I wrote my daily agenda in two sections, one for my secular role and the other for ministry projects. Admittedly, my job agenda constituted the bulk of the daily agenda, but writing the list helped me make sure God got His fair share. I use a legal-sized yellow pad, devoting a new page for every day, and write in my priority items with little notes to myself. Its size and color make it difficult to lose and it provides a valuable history of how I am spending my life. There are many excellent commercially available planning instruments. Many of the survey respondents recommended the Franklin Planner for setting goals and mapping out the daily activity agenda.

Suggestions for Writing Your Daily To-Do List

- Pick a quiet place and a quiet time the prior evening or early next morning.
- Relate your daily activities in some way to your established goals.
- Prioritize and then write all activities in order of importance.
- Do the A's first, then the B's and don't worry if you don't always get to the C's.
- Keep asking the vital question: IS THIS ACTIVITY REALLY NECESSARY?
- Be ruthless in rooting out those activities that are nice to do but totally unnecessary.
- You can't do everything there is to do today despite the demands of others.
- Try to set a time limit for each action.
- Divide and accomplish. Through the Holy Spirit, inch-by-inch everything is a cinch.
- Do all for the greater honor and glory of God.

A Promise That Delivers

If you spend five to ten minutes in planning your day you will save at least one hour or more that otherwise would be spent in unnecessary motions. That's an axiom that's almost sacrosanct among the time management mavens. I didn't believe it until I finally tried it. I hope you get in the habit of doing it too, because it really works.

Chapter Eight

DELEGATING – OR – THE DISCIPLES' DILEMMA

The Art of Letting Go

Roger Cardinal Mahony's theologian, Dr. Michael Downey, described the Cardinal's management style for me in a recent interview, "The Cardinal knows how to delegate; this is part of the reason why he accomplishes so much in his very busy ministry. But, once he has delegated an assignment, he trusts people to perform well. He doesn't look over their shoulders." The operative word here is *trust*, which means he is confident that the staff will perform well but tolerates the possibility that they may occasionally make mistakes.

Dr. R. Alec Mackenzie, author of *The Time Trap*, calls the inability to delegate "the fallacy of omnipotence — otherwise known as, 'I can do it better myself fallacy.'" It's a dead give-away that those who are guilty of this weakness are amateurs in the art of delegation.

Many of us often experience difficulty in delegating some of our authority to others, whether it relates to our secular occu-pations or ministerial roles. This is especially evident with those who are newly engaged in ministry. It afflicts the veterans too.

They just can't seem to "let go" and permit subordinates to take control of some meaningful task or project. There are many reasons for this shortsighted attitude. We may feel threatened by the abilities, creative ideas, or even the achievements of others. We may fear that by relinquishing authority we are revealing a weakness or lack of ability. We may be concerned that the subordinate will do a poor job or, God forbid, that the neophyte just might do it better. We therefore squander our time and deprive others of the opportunity to use their talents and thereby grow.

Father Thomas P. Sweetser, S.J., in his book *The Parish as Covenant — A Call to Pastoral Partnership,* states that pastors will have to establish a better balance in their daily activities if they wish to be more effective. In his chapter, "Finding a Balance — The Effective Use of Time," he suggests, "as a result of (pastors) limiting their workloads, parishes will have to supplement the ministry of the pastor with trained people who will share the pastor's duties and with empowered pastoral councils and committees to coordinate ministries and share in the decision-making. The pastor cannot and should not do it all. Others, both staff and lay leaders, are ready and willing to pick up the slack. This is a joint venture, pastors and people together." Ideally, one should voluntarily delegate as a matter of good management. If the reluctant delegator wants ministry to survive or grow he will eventually be forced to share responsibilities.

One of the saddest situations in parishes and other areas of ministry occurs when the pastor or superior restrains gifted staff members and volunteers from using their talents effectively for the good of the community. They are micromanaged to a fault. Some become so frustrated that they finally lose heart and leave the vineyard. Others endure the situation with patience until a better opportunity presents itself. I am reminded of the irate parishioner who stalked into the church office one day shouting, "I have a major complaint and I demand to see someone with a little authority around this place." "Well," replied the pastoral associate, "I have as little authority as anyone around here so you might as well speak to me."

The Moses Monopoly Mania

I think one of the best examples of the art of delegation was cited by Edwin Bliss in his book, *Getting Things Done.* He refers to the story of Moses and Jethro as it is written in Exodus 18:13-27. Moses had just led his people out of Egypt and, like many great leaders, believed he was qualified to do just about everything else. He promptly fell into the delegation trap. He appointed himself judge and jury for all manner of infractions of the law. "Moses sat to judge the people and the people stood before Moses from morning until evening" says it all. But Jethro, his shrewd father-in-law, advised Moses, "What is this thing you are doing to the people? This thing you are doing is not good. Both you and these people who are with you will wear yourselves out. For this thing is too much for you. You are not able to perform it by yourself." Jethro advised Moses to teach the Israelites the laws and statutes and then select able men to judge the people but assign the most difficult cases to himself. Jethro didn't attend Harvard Business School but he was familiar with one of the most effective management principles.

We might well honor Jethro as the first time-management consultant. His advice still applies to those of us who are unwilling to share responsibility with others in ministry. Is it any surprise that when we succumb to the "Moses Monopoly Mania," we are wearing ourselves out?

In the Gospels we see Christ as the master delegator. He directed the apostles to go forth, to heal, preach, and teach. In Luke 10:17 we learn how they returned on one occasion to report that even the demons were subject to them. Further, in John 14:12, we hear that astounding pronouncement from Christ, "Whoever believes in me will do the works that I do, he will do greater works than these, because I am going to the Father."

As we become more experienced we begin to realize that we can't do everything on our own. We eventually learn that, when we delegate duties and responsibilities to others, we can reap enormous benefits. We will save time and energy; we will accomplish much more; we will help others grow, and we will become more effective leaders.

Following are some things to keep in mind on delegation:
- Delegation doesn't diminish you.
- Delegation is not an abdication of your authority or accountability.
- Give others authority but request feedback.
- Beware false pride in your authority.
- Beware this trap: "It's easier and quicker to do it myself."
- Beware this possibility: "Others won't grow and we won't grow."
- Beware this threat: "Others just might do it better."
- Beware this danger: "Others might perform the task poorly."
- Avoid this mindset: "Politics in ministry will discourage delegation."
- Share this opportunity: "Allow others to grow."

Multiplying Your Ministry Through Others

> So shall my word be that goes forth from my mouth;
> it shall not return to me void,
> But shall do my will,
> achieving the end for which I sent it.
>
> Isaiah 55:11

I remain awed at the tremendous privilege and opportunity given to those who preach and teach the message of Christ. The typical priest, deacon, or minister may address hundreds, even thousands, at weekend services. During a ten or fifteen minute homily they sow the seed and thereby multiply within their congregation the potential for doing tremendous good. Their listeners, in turn, may spread the message to countless others. Sometimes, this *multiplier dynamic* is not that evident, or its effects may be delayed. I encountered a missionary several years ago who had returned from a six-year stint in India. "You must have made many converts to Christianity during your assignment there," I said. "No" he replied, "perhaps only one or two." He was neither apologetic nor discouraged. As a university professor he sowed the seed of faith among thousands of potential Christians. The harvest will occur in future generations when he will have passed into eternity. What a tremendous inspiration this incident should be for all of us who labor in God's vineyard, whether as clerics, teachers, or parents. We sow and cultivate for decades but will often be denied the privilege of experiencing the harvest. The miracle of the multiplication will occur nonetheless because His word "shall not return... void" (Isaiah 55:11).

Envy in Politics and Ministry

There is but one man who can believe himself
free from envy,
And it is he who has never examined his own heart.
C.A. Helvetius, *De L'esprit*, 1758

And now we move to one of the most embarrassing and
sensitive aspects of ministry. I hesitated including this topic but
I strongly believe the practice of power politics and envy
inhibits others from freely exercising their gifts and causes the
loss of enormous amounts of time. The scandal and discouragement it engenders among the faithful is sinful and may even
border on the criminal. You may see very little published about
this subject, yet it is whispered about in conferences, conclaves
and church halls, or wherever brothers and sisters of the cloth
may gather. I lump them together, both envy and politics,
because they are related and rank among the more reprehen-
sible failings that beset the Church.

The sin of envy and the scandal of political intrigue have been
with us since the founding of the Church. Remember in scripture how the Apostles were arguing among themselves about
"who was the greatest among them?" I wonder how the other
Apostles reacted when Jesus invited only Peter, James, and John
to accompany Him to Mount Tabor? And then Scripture is not
silent about Peter and Paul's frequent disagreements. Contemporary disciples are certainly no different than Christ's disciples. Witness the surprising comments of Archbishop Fulton J.
Sheen who was one of the most popular and effective church-
men of the twentieth century. In an interview conducted by
Monsignor Thomas J. Hartman in 1979, Sheen made this
remarkable disclosure, "The other type of pain, the inner one,
came to me and comes to others from pettiness and jealousy

within the Church. We do such a disservice to the Lord and our people by being envious and jealous of others. This has been the hardest cross for me to bear."

We all have, at one time or another, been victims or perpetrators of this painful practice. Why can't we rejoice in the gifts and talents of others and sincerely encourage their efforts? When I am tempted to envy the achievements of the more talented servants I try to recall the gem of wisdom offered long ago by a venerable retreat master, "Envy not your brothers and sisters who glorify God through the use of their gifts. Rather, take great consolation in realizing that you too have special, yet different, talents. You will be judged by God, not in comparison with others, but by how well you used the gifts given you."

I firmly believe that God, on that great Day of Judgment, will deal severely with those of us who have engaged in politics and practiced envy to the detriment of the faithful. The irony is that the whole world is ripe for the harvest. Why then would we interfere with those who zealously strive to reap souls for Christ? What a colossal waste of time, energy, and talent. Those who envy their colleagues in ministry may unknowingly prevent them from coming to the aid of the most desperate. Furthermore, they are diminishing the greater glory of God. P.P. Parker, a once-prominent religious author, wrote: "A man can do a great deal in this world if he doesn't mind who takes the credit." I would like to change this well-known dictum to, "A person in ministry can do or enable another to do just about anything for God — if he doesn't care who gets the credit." But it takes tons of humility and discipline for us to adhere to this standard.

Chapter Nine

THE PRICE OF PROCRASTINATION

No one who sets his hand to the plow
and looks to what was left behind
is fit for the kingdom of heaven.

Luke 9:62

We Are All Charter Members of the Procrastinators Club

An honest-to-goodness Procrastination Club of America, Inc.
does exist. It's located in Bryn Athyn, Pennsylvania. I first heard
of this organization in 1980 and my curiosity prompted me to
contact them but I never got around to it until eighteen years
later. My delay should have automatically qualified me for
immediate membership. The Club's president replied to my
inquiry six months later and enclosed an application. He also
had the chutzpah to charge a substantial fee for membership in
an organization that literally does nothing. The application still
remains in my "C" file labeled "Unimportant Things to Do."

I believe most of us are eligible members for this club. Just
think about the countless things we could have done over the
years but over which we hesitated and delayed until it was too
late.

79

Here is how some seasoned people in ministry cope with procrastination.

Fr. Joseph Champlin says, "I use a daily period of prolonged prayer, have a basic plan for the day; break large tasks into small parts; do one thing at a time."

"One must be in a ministry that he or she loves," is Sr. Mary Ann Zollman's solution to the problem of procrastination.

Deacon William Ditewig concedes procrastination poses one of his biggest challenges but suggests, "One thing I do that I do every day is to pray for wisdom, strength, and energy to do the Lord's will. When I am reminded that this is not my ministry but sharing Christ's own ministry, I find myself renewed and usually get back on track."

Reverend Thomas Krosnicki, S.V.D., Provincial, Society of the Divine Word, suggests, "get at things after they are brought to your attention. They don't get easier by leaving them to cook."

Cardinal Mahony lives by this motto, "Never let your fingers touch a paper twice." (You might try adopting this habit. You will soon discover how great a challenge it will pose.)

Difficulty in Making Decisions

There is no more miserable human being than one in whom nothing is habitual but indecision, and for whom the lighting of every cigar, the drinking of every cup, the time of rising and going to bed every day, and

the beginning of every bit of work, are subjects of express volitional deliberation.
William James, Philosopher/Psychologist (1842-1910)

The story is told about a recent President of the United States who had difficulty making up his mind. He seemed to let the national polls dictate his policy decisions. A staff member diplomatically suggested he see a professional counselor. The psychiatrist began the first session with this statement: "Mr. President, I understand you have difficulty making up your mind and then delaying most of your decisions." There followed a long painful pause. The leader of our country finally responded, "Well, yes. And — no." Then there was the confused gentleman who admitted, "I used to have difficulty making decisions — but now I'm not so sure."

The word "decide" is derived from the Latin *decidere* meaning, "to cut off," as in terminating a doubt, ending a discussion, and coming to a conclusion. It has overtones of a painful process, which it often is. Rarely do we make decisions about which we have total certainty concerning their absolute correctness. But there are methods we can use to make our decision-making activities more effective and thereby save much time and energy. Our days are filled with choices and decisions. Some experts believe the average person makes two to three hundred conscious decisions daily.

Business literature is replete with treatises that provide practical formulae to help us make good decisions in a timely fashion. I have taught and used some in my business life and found them to be practical and very effective. But when it comes to our spiritual and ministerial life I have discovered an outstanding book by Fr. Michael Scanlan, T.O.R., Past President and Chancellor of Franciscan University of Steubenville, in

Steubenville, Ohio. He outlines in his text, *What Does God Want — A Practical Guide for Making Decisions,* an approach that seems tailor-made for those of us who make daily decisions in our ministry. Fr. Scanlan calls it the "Five Step" approach to the discernment and decision-making process. He suggests that we ask ourselves these questions when attempting to make important decisions:

1. Is It in Conformity to God's Revealed Will?
   His Will is present in scripture, tradition, and the teachings of the Church.

2. Does It Encourage Conversion?
   Will it lead to holiness and a closer union with God; will it lead to a more faithful discharge of my present responsibilities?

3. Is It Consistent?
   Is it consistent with the way God led you in the past when dealing with the same people as well as with similar occasions and circumstances?

4. What Confirms It?
   Is it confirmed by those people who know me, by positive circumstances, and by the Holy Spirit?

5. Do You Have Conviction? Does the Heart Say, "Yes"?
   Do I have moral certainty; is this the right thing to do; is this the best alternative? Are there no appreciable negative consequences?

Dominant Types of Procrastinators in Ministry

For some folks, the habit of procrastination is a serious behavioral problem. But for most of us it is a habit of hesitant thinking and acting that we can readily change. It is not my intention to write a comprehensive treatise on procrastination. I do, however, want to focus on those aspects of this affliction which negatively impact on certain aspects of ministry. At first glance you might not recognize the following behaviors as masking profiles of procrastination.

THE PERFECTIONIST

God's love never looks for perfection in created beings.
He knows that it dwells in Him alone.
As He never expects perfection, He is never disappointed.
Archbishop Francois Fenelon (1657-1715)

One may ask: What do perfectionists, super-achievers, and dreamers have to do with procrastination? As you will soon discover, they are guilty of many subtle types of procrastination and the ineffective use of their time. "Be perfect as your heavenly Father is perfect" (Matthew 5:48) is a scriptural exhortation familiar to most of us. After all, isn't that a goal for which we all should strive? Absolutely. The operative word however in this context is *strive.* There is no need to detour here into an exegetical discussion of Christ's intent in this scriptural mandate. Perhaps we should accept a more realistic interpretation suggested by some scripture scholars who translate Matthew 5:48 as, "Be compassionate as my heavenly Father is compassionate."

We meet many perfectionists in ministry and we discover it is not always easy to live with them or their expectations. Archbishop John O'Connor quipped, somewhat in jest, "It's hell living with a saint." We might say the same for perfectionists. I believe the difference between being a perfectionist and striving for perfection lies in the means we use to achieve a goal.

Perhaps we can approach our goals more realistically by pursuing excellence with the hope of eventually achieving perfection in the next world. Our pursuit of perfection is not achievable in this sad world of toil and sin, but excellence is certainly within our grasp. The problem with perfectionists is that they spend an inordinate amount of time polishing and perfecting even the most minor projects. Then when it does not meet their standards they tend to put the task aside, or delay its completion until every little detail is in order.

Defining "perfection" is like defining time. It borders on the impossible. Who of us can measure exactly what constitutes absolute perfection? Who among us could agree on how the "perfect" clergyman or layperson should act or perform? But there do exist standards or criteria of excellence against which we can measure our performance.

Edwin Bliss, a time management author, suggests it is more pragmatic to settle for the "quest of excellence in contrast to the pursuit of perfection." "It is gratifying," he continues "to strive for excellence in the use of our time, and forget the Holy Grail of perfection." If you approach the various areas of ministry with the idea that everything must be perfect, then you are probably not using your time and energy effectively. A pundit once quipped that, "If a thing is worth doing it is worth doing badly." He meant, of course, that it is better to do something good, which you might do imperfectly, rather than doing nothing at all. For example, you may be faced with preparing a report, homily, or program but you keep putting it off because you think you need to conduct extensive research and analysis in order to develop the perfect product. When you finally start the project you repeatedly change your outline. You add, and then discard, various source materials, as you struggle to create only the best possible result. This may be necessary in certain cases, but most projects don't warrant the inordinate amount of time you expended. In the interim, you probably ignored equally important or even more urgent tasks. The end result is that you probably never completed the original program to your satisfaction — or anyone else's either.

Salvador Dali may have had it right when he opined, "Have no fear of perfection, because you'll never reach it." Let's look at some typical behavior patterns of the perfectionist that promote procrastination and then some methods for controlling them.

Symptoms of a Perfectionist in Ministry:

- Has a guilt complex if the task is not always done on time.
- Suffers from an inadequate self-image.
- Fear of failure deters him from even starting a project.
- Is idealistic about everything; no happy middle ground or compromise.
- Assumes the martyr mantle; is overwhelmed with even the most trivial task.
- Constantly "gilds the lily," adding extras to further improve the project.
- Considers everything important and rarely meets deadlines.
- Criticizes others who don't meet his criteria for perfection.

Some Solutions for Controlling Perfectionism:

- Admit the problem exists.
- Agree you must change yourself since you have little control over others.
- Accept oneself as "still under construction" and still imperfect for now.
- Recognize the reality that you may be wasting precious time and energy.
- Set "standards of excellence" instead of "criteria for perfection."
- Set definitive goals and specific activities to achieve them.
- Be relentless in setting time frames to complete your activities and goals.
- Faithfully follow your daily "to-do list."

In the world of business, sports, and academia, the super-achiever is looked upon as the model or idol. These heroes usually receive the most lucrative financial rewards and are publicized as icons for all to imitate. I am using the super-achiever label in its negative sense with respect to ministry. It may seem strange for us to connect the super-achiever with the malady of procrastination but the relationship becomes evident once you analyze the symptoms.

Some Symptoms:

- Chronically over-books his schedule even though he knows he can't accommodate everybody and everything.
- Identifies his self-worth more by what he does than who he is.
- Won't or can't say "No", and rarely seeks assistance.
- Takes on extreme amount of work but is unable to identify true priorities.

- Lacks self-discipline necessary to establish balance in the spiritual, physical, work, and social aspects of his life.
- Boasts about his busy schedule and the fact he never takes a vacation.
- Does a few things well, many things poorly, and some things not at all.
- Harbors a chronic guilt complex about relaxing or taking time off.

Some Solutions for Overcoming the Super-Achiever Syndrome:

- Revise the way you look at your daily agenda; view it as a challenge not a chore.
- Ask yourself the critical question: "Is this task really worth doing?"
- Anticipate inevitable glitches and have a back-up plan.
- Separate your own priorities from the demands and requests of others.
- Be careful about seeking the approval of others.
- Acknowledge the embarrassment you will experience and the consequences that will result when you take on more tasks than you can handle.
- Be faithful to your daily "to-do" list.

THE MISGUIDED VISIONARY OR DREAMER

There is a myth in some ministry circles that separate roles do exist for both dreamers and doers. I reason that people in ministry, by necessity, must assume both roles from time to time. The key problem with the total dreamer or visionary is that he is often reluctant to do those things necessary to make his vision become a reality. It is more comfortable and safer for him to live on "fantasy island" where he does not have to do the heavy lifting or follow through with all the boring details. We see dreamers in ministry who mean well but delay or are reluctant to put their vision to the test with the requisite hard work.

I once worked with a pastor who had the perfect response for misguided dreamers. Well-intentioned parishioners would approach him with, "Wouldn't it be great, Father, if we could form a committee to do such and such?" or, "I think this parish should do thus and so." The pastor would politely reply, "That sounds like a splendid idea, but I think it bears more research. Now I'd like you to research it further and submit it for discussion at our next Parish Council meeting." You can probably guess the typical responses from the dreamer. "Oh no, Father, I'm not able to do anything about it right now. I just thought you and your staff could handle this since I'm sure our community really needs and wants this project." In contrast to the dreamers, the sincere doers will accept the pastor's advice and follow through.

Some Symptoms of the Dreamer or Visionary:

- Desires life to be one long love-in or laugh-fest where everyone is euphoric and lives happily ever after.
- Believes he has been directly called to this role while others must carry out his vision.
- Fancies himself the General with the grand plan and demands that the troops must follow.
- Jumps from one grandiose project to another.
- Suggests some really bizarre or "off-the-wall" projects.

Some Methods for Re-directing the Dreamer:

- Seek counseling from peers, pastor, spiritual director, and trusted friends.
- Write out a narrative plan of action for every dream or vision; include short and long-term goals as well as strategies and deadlines to achieve them.
- Write a realistic "to-do list" first, then add the "dream list."

Some Typical Signs of This Deadly and Disabling Disease

> Of all sad words of tongue and pen the saddest are these: it might have been.
> John Greenleaf Whittier

"Coulda, Woulda, Shoulda" — we frequently use or hear these words, or similar ones, in reference to lost opportunities in the job market, investments, business, or matters of the heart. We missed out on those golden chances because we waited too long. Ask any priest or minister about his regrets in delaying that important visit to a sick or dying parishioner only to discover later that the person had passed away. How many times have we been stricken with remorse for failing to come to the aid of a family member or friend before they moved away or died?

"What might have been" is that aching lament that echoes through the minds and memories of every one of us. Wisdom lies in recognizing we can never wish away all those past events or regrets, but we can learn from them. Each time they return to gnaw at our spirit we should be aware that our only solution is to surrender the unrecoverable past to the merciful hands of God.

"Put-offitis"

One who pays heed to the wind will not sow,
and one who watches the clouds will never reap.
Ecclesiastes 11:4

Procrastination wears many masks in ministry. Consider this dialogue at a typical church committee meeting. "We need more time to deliberate; we just need more facts," declares the chairperson as the exhausted members nod their drowsy heads. At times this approach is warranted but quite often it's a strategy for indecision. Little wonder the fatigued committee members become discouraged and quietly slip away. "Put-offitis" has prevailed once more. Effective business executives rarely, if ever, have the benefit of all the facts before making a decision. The memoirs of combat Generals are replete with examples of launching effective offensives based on adequate, but rarely comprehensive, information. Professionals in all walks of life press early for the pertinent data and then execute the plan. They know that "paralysis by analysis" can slow production, kill profits, and lose battles. That's why the people who can overcome this paralysis are successful leaders. So why do we procrastinate when it comes to ministerial matters? Perhaps it's our fear of failure or disappointing others. But quite frequently it's an unreasonable desire to have every conceivable fact and figure at hand before we commit to a decision. Aneurin Bevan, the British-Welsh labor leader, identified these people when he wrote: "We know what happens to people who stay in the middle of the road, they get run over."

The Brothers "If-itis" and "But-itis"

These twin procrastination brothers constantly appear in our conversation. How often do you use them in your vocabulary?

90

- If only I had more faith, but I can't seem to increase it.
- If only my pastor, or congregation, would understand me, but that's politics.
- If only I had more time to pray, but my schedule is too hectic.
- If only I had better health, but I guess it's in the genes.
- If only I were more gifted, stronger, and dynamic, but I was never that lucky.
- If only I weren't so busy and tired, but that's the cross I must carry.
- If only my spouse were more empathetic, but her mother is just the same.
- If only I were financially independent, but I never get the breaks.

From these procrastination excuses, O Lord, deliver us!

As one sage said it, "You know you're getting old when you decide to procrastinate but never get around to it."

It Is Never Too Late

> It's never too late to start over again —
> and it's always too soon to quit.
>
> Senator Fulton Buntan

I fell in love with Francis Thompson's poem, "The Hound of Heaven" when I first read it in high school. So I memorized it and delivered it at an oratorical contest. At the time I really didn't understand much of the poem's profound meaning. The years rolled on and I returned to reading it again and again, and I still do today. It's a masterful description of our journey through life. Throughout the poem, Thompson, a London derelict and drug addict, describes how Christ, the Hound of Heaven, relentlessly pursued him. Despite his attempts to escape Christ, the poet finally relents and decides to surrender to his Divine Pursuer. I have included the poem in the Bibliography section.

Although we may have made a commitment to Christ long ago and are busily engaged in ministry, we are still prone to procrastinate. We may even attempt to flee our burdensome responsibilities. But the divine "Hound of Heaven" will not halt His chase. He will pursue us relentlessly. Take comfort in the knowledge that even though we may deny and abandon Him, He will never abandon us. We can dissemble and delay but a certain catharsis occurs when we acknowledge we cannot escape the promptings of the Holy Spirit. Until we surrender we will never experience genuine peace. So, if procrastination is one of your problems in ministry, don't put off doing something about it now. As William Shakespeare wrote: "Our doubts are traitors, and make us lose the good we oft might win by fearing to attempt."

Chapter Ten

MAJORING IN MINORS AND MISSING THE MAIN MESSAGE

Blind guides, you strain out the gnat
and swallow the camel.

Matthew 23:24

Some men die by the sword
And others go down in flames
But most men perish inch by inch
In play and little games.

Abramson

Becoming Mired In Minutiae

A New England newspaper once reported that over 200 whales, a species well-known for their intelligence, were chasing schools of sardines, but for some strange reason left the deep waters and pursued those tiny creatures into a shallow bay. Tragically, they became stranded there when the tide went out and they eventually died. They were lured to their destruction while pursuing trivial ends.

Why do we chase after minutiae and become marooned in fruitless activities? It's a universal but perverse part of our human nature. President Lyndon Johnson, who reputedly enabled the passage of more legislation than any prior President, was famous for his ability to focus completely on the major issues. When members of the Congress tried to steer his agenda into minor projects, he responded, "The trouble with our country is that we constantly put second things first." People in ministry certainly are not immune from this tendency. Honestly examine your own pastoral agenda or list of projects, programs, and pet pursuits in which you ask your congregations to be involved. Then, ask the tough questions. "How necessary are they? Is this really the most important project of all possible programs? What will this do to help people find Christ?"

The Eagle Catches No Flies

I used to help conduct management seminars in Chicago's prestigious Drake Hotel. I recall the exquisite dinnerware used for the business banquets. Inscribed on the dishes, bowls, cups, and saucers was the epigram, "Aquila Muscas Non Captat," meaning "An Eagle Catches No Flies." I once asked the headwaiter if he knew the translation. "Yeah," he replied, "'Don't sweat the small stuff.' Management probably put it there to impress their business clientele." Think about it for a minute, how much time do you spend "chasing and catching flies" or "sweating the small stuff"? I repeatedly ask myself these same questions, "Why do we so easily get mired down in the minutiae of ministry? Why do we permit ourselves to be detoured into the byways of meaningless activities?" We probably do so, in large measure, because we failed to set meaningful goals or tend to ignore them. It's easier and more pleasurable to involve ourselves in the less demanding and more attractive projects.

We fool others and ourselves into thinking that being busy at "being busy" is still a productive use of our time. C. Northcote Parkinson, the British political scientist, was on the mark when he wrote: "We tend to devote more time and effort to tasks in inverse relation to their importance."

The Rev. Dennis Maynard, the founding pastor of St. Martin's Episcopal Church in Houston, Texas, tells the following story of how he was invited back to the church for the 25th anniversary of the parish. And one by one, folks came up to him and said, "You married us and baptized our children." "Do you remember that sermon you preached on forgiveness? It really moved me." "Do you remember when you came to the hospital to baptize our baby?" "When I was having a tough time you gave me this copy of the Serenity Prayer Book. I still have it." "You gave me this article. It helped me through my divorce." But the pastor's own reminiscences were met with blank looks. He recited his own litany of "brilliant ideas" which had consumed his time and energy as a pastor. But while the programs had been a source of great pride for him, they were not part of the collective memory of the congregation. Reverend Maynard concludes, "That which made a difference in the lives of the people I served was not my brilliant program ideas, strategic plans or my efforts to impress them with my leadership and management skills… what they remembered was not my brilliance, but those moments when I got out of the way and God touched them."

Perhaps this incident should give us pause and help us put our ministry priorities in perspective. Are we sometimes missing the main message of our ministry? The poor, the parishioners who are hurting, the unemployed, the homeless, and the abandoned are trying to tell us something. Are we listening to them and addressing their real needs? Why wait until our retirement dinner to discover belatedly that some of our *important programs* and *pet projects* were not that important after all. Cardinal Bernardin wrote to his priests just before he died, "Get away from paperwork. Ask yourself, when people come to church are they finding Jesus? If they are not, then they are wasting their time." I might add that we are wasting our time too.

Fr. Mychal Judge, the Capuchin assigned to St. John's Church on West 31st Street in Manhattan, was the first official casualty in the World Trade Center disaster on September 11, 2001. As a New York City Fire Department Chaplain he ministered to firefighters and their families. But the poor, the homeless, the addicts, and the forgotten of Manhattan were his primary parishioners. According to his biographer, Michael Ford, Fr. Judge had the gift of being exclusively present to each person to whom he ministered. They had the distinct impression that this friar was only interested in them when he wanted to help them. Judge was neither a saint nor a perfectionist. I liked Ford's comment that Judge embodied the spirit of Thornton Wilder's maxim, "In God's army only the wounded may serve." Judge was keenly aware of his imperfections but these failings did not deter him as he relentlessly pursued his main mission: to devote every hour of every day in ministering to parishioner, friend, stranger, and everyone whom he encountered. It was evident that Mychal Judge was in love with his ministry and love is the reason for success in any ministry. In his book, *The Rhythm of Life,* Matthew Kelly writes, "The legends, heroes, leaders, champions, and saints that fill our history books loved what they did. People of this caliber dedicate their whole being to their pursuits." He continues, "This is the Dedication Principle — *In order to love what you do, you must do what you love.*"

This following story may sound apocryphal, but an acquaintance solemnly swears he worked with a fellow laborer in the Lackawanna, N.Y. Steel Plant, which once employed as many as 25,000 workers. For years his colleague would wander all day throughout the vast complex of rolling and strip mills, wearing an unauthorized supervisor's helmet, clipboard in hand, and looking very official indeed. His boss, who was distracted with other projects, told him to "just look busy." And he did exactly that for several years, but did little else. Other workers assumed he was a person of importance and he gradually deluded himself in thinking the same. It was rumored that eventually he was promoted to a supervisor of sorts because he "just looked the part." But in ministry "just looking the part" will not cut it. People will soon discover when we only "talk the talk" but fail to "walk the walk."

Beware "The Activity Trap"

George Odiorne, a management guru, coined the phrase "The Activity Trap." "This Trap," he writes, "is that abysmal situation people find themselves in when they start pursuing what was once an important objective, but in an amazingly short time become so enmeshed in the activity of getting there that they forgot where they were going." Does this description fit any of the programs in which you have become trapped? How many committees take on a life of their own, as the well-intentioned flounder around in the bottomless "activity trap"? We should not be surprised when we develop a healthy distrust for those never-ending meetings and committees. When it comes to our spiritual life we can spend countless hours in *holy activities* without ever achieving real holiness.

Some of our modern youth have become disaffected with organized religion because they claim, and with some validity, that our churches are one vast collection of laws, rules, and regulations. They allege some of our leaders are like the Pharisees of old in that they confuse form with real substance. It's that old "Activity Trap" again. Are we missing the main message by preaching and practicing the inconsequential and meaningless?

Ralph Martin, in his book *Unless the Lord Build the House*, expressed his concerns about fruitless religious activities. "So many of our programs, structures, courses, sermons, are 'of the flesh, of the will of man.'… The frightening judgment is that they produce no fruit. Only what is of the Spirit produces life. What does it avail us, all our budgets and programs and councils? Nothing, unless they be of the Spirit of God."

Applying Alfredo Pareto's Law To Ministry

Alfredo Pareto, an eminent 19th century sociologist, discovered that if all items or activities were arranged in the order of their value, 80% of the value would derive from only 20% of the activities. The remaining 20% of the value would come from 80% of the activities. This phenomenon is commonly known as the 80/20 rule. Incidentally, I do suspect that it could be changed to the 90/10 rule when applied to some church related activities.

I have seen, firsthand, how this formula operated in sales organizations. Astute sales managers realize that ultimately 80% of all sales, regardless of the product, are produced by 20% of their sales force. They also know that a mere 20% of their customer base generates 80% of total sales volume.

Which group of salespeople and customers do you think managers will focus on in a special way? I have yet to hear of anyone attempting to apply this well-established formula to ministry. Yet, I submit that both in theory and practice we can apply the 80/20 rule to many of our ministry activities. Our challenge, then, lies in identifying those top 20% of goals and activities that will help us achieve 80% of the benefits. In Chapter 5 you identified your priority goals. Logically those goals and their related activities should produce 80% of the value of all your ministry actions. Determining the goals and activities that will give you the 80% of benefits for those whom you serve is a constant process. But it can produce staggering results.

Be Both Effective and Efficient

> There is nothing so useless
> as doing efficiently
> what should not be done at all.
> Peter Drucker

Peter Drucker, one of America's foremost management experts, succinctly explained the difference between efficiency and effectiveness. "Effectiveness" he said, "is doing the right job, whereas efficiency is doing the job right." Our aim should be to choose the right project from all other possibilities and then perform that project in the correct manner. The automobile industry isn't alone in producing Edsels. We, in ministry, produce our own versions. How often have you observed or produced a wonderfully planned program, only to see it fail because your expected audience showed little interest or enthusiasm? It proved ineffective because it did not meet the perceived needs of the potential audience. We compound the debacle when we refuse to admit our error in judgment and are unwilling to shelve our project which proved to be ineffective and of benefit to no one. As a Southern minister quipped, "Some dogs just won't hunt."

Chapter Eleven

HOW TO SAVE TWO HOURS A DAY

Walk not as unsure men but as wise,
making the most of time.
Ephesians 5:15

The title of this chapter may sound similar to those dubious promises headlining the tabloids at the supermarket checkout counter. I don't promise to give you additional hours, but I will show you how to make several hours available so you can do more important things. This really means you will be trading off one activity for another.

Kicking the TV Habit

In January of 1976 a football fanatic returned home from church with his family. After breakfast he promptly plopped down in front of the television set. His buddies then arrived and there they sat, staring at the film footage of Super Bowls past. His wife served lunch and they continued lounging throughout the afternoon, shouting and cheering as the Super Bowl progressed. His friends eventually went home and his wife and children retired for the night. But he remained transfixed before the boob tube listening to countless commentators repeating what he had been watching for hours.

As I finally turned off that idiot box, after fourteen hours of mindless viewing, I was consumed with guilt over this colossal waste of time. There and then I vowed not to watch television for one year. I kept that promise. The rewards proved to be enormously gratifying. Did I miss T.V.? You bet I did. But instead, I read at least one book a week, spent more quality time with my family, and even earned a promotion at work. I experienced a renewed surge of willpower that arises when one overcomes an addictive habit. Did I ever return to watching T.V.? Yes, but on a very selective basis. That habit of self-control remains to this day.

Sometimes we have to go "cold turkey" to kick some bad habits. The average person who watches television can easily save one to two hours a day by simply being more selective. If we completely abstain we will free up a treasure trove of time. We can then spend this "saved" time on those important things for which we never seemed to have enough time. One approach is to anticipate the pleasure you will experience in reading, writing, or performing another project. Gradually, you will find yourself busily occupied with so many more important pursuits that you will have soon forgotten the lure of the "trivia tube." It's the art of substitution. We replace a less desirable habit with something pleasurable and more beneficial.

"Computeritis" and its Consequences

Then there is that magnificent communication machine, the computer, which is so rapidly changing the world. Its benefits and timesaving economies are startling, but the time-wasting possibilities are frightening. I finally entered the computer world late in life. I soon recognized it as a valuable gift as well as a potential curse. Sending and receiving e-mail alone can consume several precious hours daily, not to mention time dedicated to surfing the Internet. Your use of the computer is a very subjective decision. I want to impress upon you that a very powerful giant now lives with us and works for us or against us. We alone must determine if it will be our slave or master. I limit myself to one hour daily, unless I'm involved in a project. I have to guard against this useful tool becoming an addictive toy.

Do I Really Need To Read That?

That is the first question we need to ask when we are confronted with tons of reading material. Over 165,000 new book titles are published every year in the U.S. and Canada. There are in excess of one million titles in print and another 100 million in the Library of Congress. We are awash in literature of every variety, ranging from the inspiring to the trashiest novels one can imagine. The volume of new texts in the religious and spiritual market is growing exponentially. Publishers are beginning to realize people are hungry for ideas that feed the soul and nourish the spirit. There are so many newspapers, magazines, and books that we would love to read but we can usually find time for only the most important. Just look around your house or office at all the books you have yet to read and the ones you promised years ago you would read again. We need to adopt a disciplined selection process. Astute business people read succinct summaries of business and world news. We can access, in the same manner, what is most important in the spiritual and religious publishing world through weekly synopses services. I find it helpful to check with my colleagues in ministry to learn what current reading material they consider both interesting and helpful.

Capitalizing On Our Commuter and Waiting Time

> Lost, yesterday, somewhere between sunrise and sunset,
> Two golden hours, each set with sixty golden minutes.
> No reward is offered, for they are gone forever.
>
> Horace Mann

I once worked for a gentleman who, for thirty years, commuted two-and-a-half hours each way from Philadelphia to Manhattan on a daily basis. Many of his colleagues told him it was sheer madness. Arthur simply smiled in response. He completed at least 80% of his daily work agenda during those precious five hours on the buses and trains. He would arrive at the office with a file full of notes and ideas that he and I would then develop into programs and conferences. We spent the afternoons interviewing busy executives and testing Arthur's brainstorms. He generated those profit-making ideas on his long train ride while others slept, read or played cards. He taught me a powerful lifetime lesson that I still try to apply every day.

We have many options when we travel or commute. Admittedly, for safety reasons, we are limited when driving an automobile, but that doesn't preclude listening to tapes, praying, or practicing an upcoming presentation. I am writing this chapter while waiting for a plane in the West Palm Beach, Florida airport. Yes, it was delayed for several hours. I could have chosen to stew and fret over the delay but I decided to do something that was both pleasurable and productive.

Let's face it, for the rest of our lives we will consume precious time traveling as well as waiting, waiting, waiting. We can reduce and control our traveling hours but we can never entirely eliminate this inconvenience unless we happen to be Trappist monks who are fortunate in having solved this problem. Those chunks of time are like precious pearls scattered throughout our day just waiting for us to pick them up, use them wisely, or just pass them by.

> I have only just a minute
> Only sixty seconds in it
> Forced upon me, can't refuse it
> But it's up to me to use it.
> I must suffer if I lose it
> Give account if I abuse it
> Just a tiny little minute
> But eternity is in it.
> ("Just A Minute", Anonymous)

Some Secrets of the Saints and Folks like Us

> Great occasions for serving God come seldom,
> but little ones surround us daily.
> St. Francis de Sales

> Time for St. John Neumann was the coin of eternity
> and the most careful stewardship
> had to be exercised over every moment.
> John Cardinal Krol

> I have made a solemn promise to God
> that I will never waste a minute.
> St. Alphonsus Liguori

"I use the 'small moments' effectively," writes Sr. Zollman. "Some projects take a large block of creative time and so, while in a few moments here and there I cannot attend to those, I have at hand smaller projects — a simple phone call, a brief note, a review of minutes — and I do those in the 'little moments.'" A good part of our daily routine consists of prolonged segments of activity with some brief intervening snippets of time. We may delude ourselves into thinking that we don't have enough time to do any meaningful tasks during those short breaks as we await our next appointment, event, or daily chore. While we wait, time ticks away and those minutes, like grains of sand, slip through our idle hands.

During World War I, Fr. Willie Doyle, a Jesuit Army Chaplain, kept a daily diary while he ministered to the troops on the front battle lines. In the diary he wrote how he was able to whisper an incredible number of short prayers and aspirations. It was his way of "praying unceasingly." In this manner, whether during the fiercest fighting or in times of rest at the rear, Doyle was able to experience the "presence of God." He was probably whispering these prayers when he was killed in Flanders while ministering to his soldiers.

It may seem impractical for us to try to emulate Chaplain Doyle but we might develop our own practice of praying during those brief intervals which occur during our daily routine. I fill some of my "spare moments" by reciting a favorite aspiration. It's called the Jesus Prayer, "O Lord Jesus Christ, Son of God, have mercy on me a sinner." I have prayed this ancient mantra over the years and it has never failed to calm me, no matter the crisis or problem. Part of this Jesus Prayer is derived from Luke 18:13 in the Parable of the Pharisee and the Tax Collector: "All he did was beat his breast and say, 'O God, be merciful to me, a sinner.'" Scripture experts advise that the original Greek translation reads *the* sinner not *a* sinner, thus emphasizing that the contrite tax collector identified himself not simply as one sinner among many but the *sinner par excellence.*

106

How To Conduct Effective and Efficient Meetings

> Work expands to fill the time available
> in which to do the work.
> C. Northcote Parkinson

An old fable relates that, when God was creating the animal kingdom, a group of curious angels remarked that it seemed like a lot of fun. They pleaded with God to let them participate in a creation committee. God hesitated, but then relented and permitted the angels to join in the process. They began to argue and negotiate for hours on end. Finally, they produced their first animal and named the poor creature a platypus — an animal with the bill of a duck, the tail of a beaver, the feet of a frog, and the fur of an otter. "Enough already," God shouted. And from that moment onward there were no more committees in heaven.

But committees still endure here on earth and where there are committees there will always be meetings, too many of them. Time management consultants believe 50% of all meetings are either unnecessary or unproductive. You may well recall the many meetings you convened or attended that went on for hours. You left these sessions having accomplished little or nothing other than producing a group of exhausted and frustrated people. Little wonder some of these disillusioned volunteers never return for round two. It amazes me why otherwise intelligent participants, who surely must follow disciplined meeting strategies in their places of business, seem to abandon the rules when they are involved in church-related meetings. So why do we put up with it? Some pastors argue that they have to coax and cajole volunteers to attend a meeting in the first place and are reluctant to play the martinet in over-controlling the session. But there should be no mystery about conducting interesting and effective meetings. Well-run businesses have perfected the process so let's adopt their strategies in our ministry.

Refer to Exhibit 5, *How To Conduct Effective and Efficient Meetings*, and Exhibit 6, *Meeting Minutes Summary*, each located in the Appendix at the end of this book. These represent a distillation of the many techniques I have seen used over the years. You may wish to duplicate or modify them and use them at your next meeting, then watch how your sessions will improve and people will feel more productive. We should treat committee members or meeting participants like professionals. They, in turn, will respect you and participate more positively.

I always try to start meetings exactly on time despite warnings like, "In our parish or in this group it's been the custom to begin 10 to 15 minutes late." You will irk some with your new approach but the word soon gets around and the sessions start improving. Prepare for your next session by following the steps in Exhibit 5 and conclude the meeting with Exhibit 6, *The Meeting Minutes Summary*.

I used to have difficulty ending meetings on time primarily because of sidebar conversations and general socializing. A clever moderator showed me how to correct this by simply making the following request, "I respect your desire to converse with your friends or engage in social dialogue, but in fairness to all, let's complete our agenda and then we can have optional time for conversation and refreshments." It's just another way to win friends and help guarantee the success of the session.

Chapter Twelve

FOR EVERYTHING THERE IS A TIME

There is an appointed time for everything
and a time for every purpose under heaven.
Ecclesiastes 3:1

Timing is Almost Everything

Success happens when certain positive critical factors or events converge at the proper time. I believe that of all the necessary components that must come to bear to produce a successful outcome, timing is the most important. Hence timing is almost, but not quite, everything. We see this dynamic develop in events as disparate as political elections, military conflicts, baseball world series, and even automobile accidents. And it works the same way in our world of ministry. All the strategies we employ to produce certain programs just won't cut it unless they satisfy specific needs at the proper time.

Don't you admire those folks in ministry who have that uncanny knack of always doing the right thing at the right time? Most programs which they conduct seem to be perfectly appropriate for the people's needs. We know this is not purely due to luck or happenstance. These experts apparently are veteran practitioners of sound management principles. They are disciplined in the art of good planning, organizing, goal setting, implementing, and controlling. What appears for them to be an effortless and flawless production is the result of intense effort behind the scenes. Just as impressive is their ability to make the project or event happen at the right time. We too can learn that skill of proper timing if we are willing to adopt the same successful techniques used by the experts.

I always yearned to be an entrepreneur. My first opportunity came in 1967. I had spent several years with the American Management Association in New York City when I finally decided to take the leap into the world of the independent businessman. Two publisher friends and I formed a small consulting firm. We leased a cubbyhole office on Madison Avenue in New York City, issued pretentious press releases, called ourselves Management Seminars Inc., and in their infinite wisdom, my partners named me President. We developed and conducted seminars and conferences for the insurance and financial services industry. We became successful beyond our most optimistic expectations — at least for the first few years. One day I convinced my partners that we had to diversify in order to grow. So I designed an ambitious series of seminars entitled, *"HOW TO SURVIVE IN THE STOCK MARKET."* What did I know about the Stock Market? Absolutely nothing! I interviewed dozens of well-known Wall Street mavens, picked their brains, and convinced many of them to participate as speakers at our nationally advertised conference. "But John," my partners pleaded, "let's re-think this project. We are sailing into uncharted waters and the time is just not right."

But I sailed on. Flushed with the euphoria of past successes, I contracted for an $18,000 advertisement in the *Wall Street*

Journal. But the advertisement did not appear until the very day of the conference. We had been "bumped" in favor of the Journal's institutional advertisers. We had already mailed several thousand brochures to potential attendees. Our fifteen speakers promptly appeared at the prestigious Waldorf Astoria Hotel — to speak to a mere 15 attendees, not the 300 to 400 we had confidently expected. Did I blow it big time? You bet. To the tune of over $40,000. My timing was atrocious. I still keep the seminar brochure as a sober reminder of "Flanagan's Folly." Incidentally, the Dow Jones dropped over 800 points that week and the recession began in earnest. Timing is almost everything!

I have seen church-related ventures fail for some of these same reasons. Wise leaders in ministry do not rely on their own judgment before launching a mission. They do an in-depth survey of their respective community. They will do the required research to determine what the flock needs and wants and then, most importantly, decide the most appropriate time to introduce the program.

Pace Yourself — Make Haste Slowly

"Festina Lente!" our Latin professor, Fr. August Loechte, would announce as we rushed our recitation in translating the "Caesar's Gallic Wars" assignment. *"Make Haste Slowly,"* he would explain when he saw our puzzled looks. To fourteen-year-olds his comment made about as much sense in English as it did in Latin. The patient professor then went on to point out that several good things would happen when we took time to carefully and correctly translate those mysterious Latin phrases. We would save time in the end since we would not have to go

back and revise our original sloppy translations. We could take pride in doing the job correctly in the first place. I'm sure the professor also realized that we rushed the recitation hoping he would not notice our mispronunciations and terrible translations.

"God made time but men made haste," is an ancient maxim. The speed mania is pervasive everywhere in our culture. Unfortunately we equate efficiency with speed, but rapidity of motions is only one component of effective activity. In the ministry arena I refer to these speed merchants as those *Whirling Divine Dervishes.* Perhaps they never heard of *making haste slowly.* You see them rushing from one project to another, overwhelming themselves and everyone else. When asked how she was able to bury 40,000 people in her lifetime, Mother Teresa replied, "I accomplished it by doing just one at a time." John Wesley frequently exhorted his followers, "Beware of trying to do too much, because you will be doing nothing [of value]." Multi-tasking has recently become one of the rages in certain productivity circles. But its future remains extremely doubtful according to many efficiency consultants. Multi-tasking means that employees attempt to do multiple activities or one or more repetitive motions simultaneously. One wit observed that multi-tasking means lousing up several things at once. In my opinion, few activities in ministry lend themselves to this experimental approach in ministry. Newly released results of scientific studies indicate that carrying on several duties at once may, in fact, reduce productivity, not increase it.

For Everything There Is a Time

"The Hurrieder I Go The Behinder I Get"

When I drive through the beautiful Amish countryside in Eastern Pennsylvania, I am always impressed with the Amish people's slow but purposeful and productive lifestyle. "The Hurrieder I Go, The Behinder I Get," is one of their many popular proverbs which we should display in our offices and meeting rooms as a constant reminder to slow down.

I once reported to an executive who was very successful and popular — except for one almost fatal flaw. We called him "Hurry Henry." When junior staff members, and sometimes his equals, entered his office, usually with appointments, he would continue writing, answer his telephone, or otherwise be engaged, and at the same time try to carry on an indirect conversation with his visitors. He was sending a distinct signal that the visitor was not really that important. His unspoken message to us was, "Don't you realize how important and busy an executive I am?" Eventually, his discouraged staff members and colleagues resorted to communicating to him only by brief written reports or voice-mail messages. They began to isolate him. Perhaps this was his peculiar time-management technique, but it didn't do much to create effective communications or good morale with his team members. Our overly busy demeanor and preoccupied manner may also cause those we serve to label us "Hurry Henrys."

Igor Stravinsky was a disciplined composer who adhered to a rigid work schedule carefully laid out in advance. Every minute of every day was taken up by some specific task. On one occasion, his publisher asked him to hurry the completion of one work. "I'm sorry," the composer said, "I haven't time in my schedule to hurry." Hurrying is the result of poor planning and usually results in doing the job in a shoddy manner.

113

When we schedule an appointment for someone to visit us we owe him the courtesy to be wholly present to him. Sometimes when parishioners telephone for an appointment or come to my office with a specific need they will preface their call with this apology, "I'm sorry to take your time. I realize you are very busy." I try to respond, "Right now I intend to be busy with you." My willingness to be available and present to them, and telling them just that, often proves to be the beginning of the healing process or the solution to their problem. It also usually shortens the duration of the meeting. After all, being available, present, and accessible to people in need, is our ministry. They are not an interruption. They are the reason for our being in the business for God.

I like Fr. Champlin's rather creative approach to interruptions: "There is a way of dealing with people who either stop in unexpectedly, interrupt our work with a telephone call, or ask us on the street about something. It basically means, right at the start, making a contract with these people and engaging in this conversation, 'I was not expecting you today but welcome you. However, I have another obligation and I can give you ten minutes right now. If we cannot take care of it in ten minutes, then we can make the time when you can come in and in a more leisurely way we can talk about this.'"

I also am impressed with the manner in which a colleague of mine begins the conversation when I answer his telephone calls. He very diplomatically begins, "Is this a convenient time for us to talk?" He respects my time and I admire his courtesy which sometimes prompts me to continue the conversation even though I may be very busy. At other times I explain my situation and then agree to return his call at a more convenient time. Try this approach and enjoy the positive results.

Chapter Thirteen

THE SECOND GREAT SECRET — THE SACRAMENT OF THE MOMENT

> The surest method of arriving
> at a knowledge of God's eternal purpose for us
> is to be found in the right use of the present moment.
> Each hour comes with some little bundle,
> which is God's will,
> fastened on its back.
>
> Fr. Frederick Faber

Practicing the Constant Presence of God

We referred in Chapter 3 to the "First Great Secret" in managing our time and talent for God, *the power of the Holy Spirit.* We will understand this "First Great Secret" when we realize we can perform incredible things through that power as long as we are doing the Will of God.

I refer now to the "Second Great Secret." There really should be no mystery surrounding this truth since it is so simple and so ancient a practice in the annals of spirituality. Simply put, it is constantly practicing the presence of the Holy Trinity in our hearts or being aware of the Indwelling of the Father, Son, and Holy Spirit.

Throughout most of his life, Nicholas Hermann of Lorraine, France, faithfully practiced this spiritual exercise which is also known as the "Sacrament of the Moment." Nicholas Hermann is better known as Brother Lawrence, who was a Carmelite lay brother, and lived during the 17th century. Lawrence was neither a theologian nor a philosopher, yet upon discovering this tremendous truth he wrote: "Practicing the constant presence of God, in my opinion, contains the whole spiritual life." He further wrote: "Were I a preacher, I should, above all things, preach the practice of the presence of God; and were I a spiritual director, I should advise all the world to do it, so necessary do I think it, and easy too." Our homilists could do well to accept Lawrence's advice.

Here we have a humble lay brother who learned this invaluable lesson of spirituality and the perfect use of his time, which even some of the most brilliant Christian writers have failed to explore. Furthermore, Brother Lawrence learned well the essence of stewardship for the Lord. He was able to grasp the significant truth that our careers, professions, roles in life, talents, and good works are secondary in importance compared to putting ourselves in the presence of God as we minister for Him.

As a humble steward serving in the monastery scullery he described his attitude toward his job. "The time of business does not differ with me from the time of prayer. And in the noise and clatter of my kitchen, while serving other persons and at the same time calling for different things, I possess God in as great a tranquility as if I were on my knees before the Blessed Sacrament."

A Time for Formal Prayer

> Until you are convinced
> that prayer is the best use of your time,
> You will not find time for prayer.
>
> Hilary Ottensmeyer, OSB

We also need time for formal prayer. In the summer of 1979, I wrote a letter to Archbishop Fulton J. Sheen asking him to share his secret on how he manages his time and talents so effectively in ministry. He wrote in reply: "In my book, *Those Mysterious Priests*, you will find a development of the idea that I have used for sixty years, in managing a busy life and allowing time for God, namely, the Holy Hour." In his book, Sheen credits this practice of spending two hours each morning before the Blessed Sacrament as the source of his spiritual strength. It is related that lay volunteers in Mother Teresa's formation houses must spend two hours early each morning in meditation and formal prayer in the Chapel. The world stands in awe at the charitable works performed by Mother Teresa's followers. But be assured those hours they spend in prayer is their secret source of strength and perseverance. John Wesley revealed how he was able to perform such prodigious works: "I have so much to do that I must spend several hours a day in prayer before I am able to do it." Both John Paul II and Mother Teresa have commented that the more they had to do in a day, the more time they would take to pray.

Ultimately, then, what is the best way for you and me to use our time and talent for the Lord? Above all, it involves our trying to be aware of God's constant presence in what we say and do. We also need to dedicate a special time of our busy schedules to formal prayer. This may sound impossible for many of us but it is a learned habit that we surely can develop even if it takes our lifetime.

That Sweet Seductive Song

There is that sweet seductive siren song that can distract and lure us into worldly pursuits. It sometimes shouts, but usually whispers, its subtle message in television, radio, books, and other news media: "You will go around but once, so grab as much pleasure and money as possible; look out for number one, eat, drink, and be merry for you will be a long time dead." Or that classic bumper sticker: "He who dies with the most toys wins." This siren song of selfishness and instant gratification permeates the films and music lyrics directed toward youthful audiences but they can affect adults as well. The Holy Spirit, that "quiet violence," relentlessly whispers: "You shall indeed pass this way but once. Use every precious day and hour for the honor and glory of God. The gift of time which I now give you is your eternity begun."

Recurring Fear — a Reassuring Hope

A certain fear sometimes comes to me in a dream. It may even haunt me during the quiet moments of the day. My fear is this: I may never get another chance if I fail now to continue responding to Christ's invitation to serve. Will I persevere in dedicating my time and talent for Him? How often will the Lord "call me by name and tell me He has need of me"? There are millions yet unborn whom He will surely call, and many will generously respond. But will I continue to do so?

Francis Thompson, in his poem *The Hound of Heaven,* describes those precious moments of grace when the trumpet call arouses us to the reality of the moment and reminds us of that need to continue doing God's work.

> I dimly guess what Time in mists confounds;
> Yet ever and anon a trumpet sounds
> From the hid battlements of Eternity;
> Those shaken mists a space unsettle, then
> Round the half glimpsed turrets then slowly wash again.
> But not ere him who summoneth
> I first have seen, enwound
> With glooming robes purpureal, cypress-crowned;
> His name I know, and what his trumpet saith.

All of us, at times, will lose sight of our goals. We become fatigued and forget how to manage our time and many talents. We need to take time out, and if we listen carefully we also will hear that trumpet call of grace as we briefly glimpse that small window into eternity. The clouds of doubt and discouragement will soon begin to dissipate and eventually fade away.

You Too Shall Be Renewed

> I will restore for you the years the locusts have eaten.
> Joel 2:25

This unusual promise, spoken through the prophet Joel, has been a source of continued inspiration for me over the years, especially when I slip into that dangerous trap called "Too Late." One of the hope-filled interpretations of this scriptural verse describes how the locusts of sin, dissipation, and abuse may have eroded the years of our lives, but God will restore to us those wasted years, perhaps not in quantity but surely in quality. I think this is one of the loveliest passages in the Old Testament because it is a message of hope. We hear people bemoan the loss of those precious years of their youth and mid-life which they squandered away in mindless pleasure. As remorse eats away at their spirit they rationalize that it is now too late to change, thus guaranteeing they will not. They reject the chance to change during those remaining years which might otherwise be the most fruitful and fulfilling of their lives.

In his reflection on the "lost years" of his youth and early manhood, St. Augustine penned these famous lines: "So late have I loved You, O Lord, so late." Note that Augustine did not say "Too late." Despite his remorse over his wasted and sinful years he reinforces the message of the Gospel and belief of spiritual writers that it is never too late to repent and change. He regretted his years of dissipation and sin but compensated for them throughout the rest of his life. So let go of those "locusts" in your own life and forget the regrets you may still harbor. I am fond of Fulton Sheen's advice, "It does not take much time to make us saints, it only requires much love."

Carpe Diem — Now is The Acceptable Time

> Behold, now is a very acceptable time;
> behold now is the day of salvation.
> 2 Corinthians 6:2

I try to exercise in a fitness center several times a week. I am amused by the variety of lettered T-shirts which many members wear. One young woman had the popular label, *Carpe Diem,* emblazoned on the back of her shirt. "Interesting shirt," I remarked while waiting my turn for the treadmill. "Do you know what it means?" I continued. "Not at all, but it sure starts a lot of conversations," she replied. "Seize the day — grasp the moment," I explained. "That is really awesome," she smiled. The precious gift of time is indeed awesome. Why not seize this very moment to decide how you will make just one change in your life in managing your time and talent for the Lord.

All Things Are Possible

> For human beings it is impossible, but not for God.
> All things are possible for God.
>
> Mark 10: 27

Self-Help and How-To books will continue to flood the marketplace as long as people sincerely desire to improve their lives. Some of these well-intentioned authors will proclaim the ease and convenience with which one can lose weight, grow rich, regain health, or become instantly successful. Many readers may succumb to the lure of the instant solution to their quest. When those promised results fail to readily materialize they become mightily disillusioned.

I have tried to be candid and very practical in this book. Most of my observations and advice are based on my lived experiences or those of informed colleagues. It is my hope that you have come to realize there is no easy formula or quick-fix approach when it comes to the stewardship of your time and talents in your chosen ministry. But all things are possible for you who love the Lord and sincerely seek to do His will.

The Myth: There is Time Enough

Following is an adaptation of an old story told and retold at evangelical revival meetings. (I have searched unsuccessfully to identify the original author.)

One night a man had a troublesome dream in which he beheld Satan seated on his throne and holding court with all his minions. He rose and shouted this question: "Who among you will go upon the earth and destroy souls?" "I will, Master," quickly replied a follower. "And what will you tell those creatures?" "I will announce that there is no God, for He is dead." "That is nonsense," responded Satan, with disgust. "Most men intuitively know there is a Supreme Being. They may deny it to their fellowmen, but in their heart of hearts they know there is a God, and some day they will be judged by Him. When sickness and suffering strikes, and as they face death, it will be difficult for them to deny their God. No, your approach will surely fail."

Satan once more bellowed out the question, "Is there no one here who can go forth to destroy mortal souls?" "I will, Master," volunteered another demon. "And what will you tell them?" "Master, I will tell them there indeed is a God, but because of their many sins He can never forgive them and they will despair." "That is equally ridiculous," replied Satan. "Their desperation will force them to seek God's forgiveness. If they read or hear Scripture they will surely know that He is a God of mercy and compassion."

And once more the challenge rang out in those halls of Hell, "Who is brave and wise enough to go forth and ruin souls for me?" A wizened old demon approached and announced, "I will, Master. I will tell them there certainly is a God. I will also assure them that He is all merciful and forgiving, but I will also tell them, THERE IS TIME ENOUGH! There is time enough to seek God and His forgiveness and time enough to change their lives." Satan applauded the demon's answer and there followed a thunderous approval from all the assembled demons. "Go forth, all of you," commanded Satan, "and tell them there will always be time enough, and you will be incredibly successful." And from that day to this they continue to spread that lie to the entire world that there is time enough to change their lives, to seek forgiveness, and to accept salvation.

But my dear readers, when it comes time to change our lives and manage our time and talents more effectively for the Lord, THERE IS NOT TIME ENOUGH. The time for change is now, for now is the acceptable time.

APPENDIX

Exhibit 1
MY GOALS FOR GOD AND STRATEGIES TO ACHIEVE THEM

"Walk not as unsure men but as wise,
making the most of time."

Ephesians 5:15

THREE-MONTH GOALS

Goal 1.

Goal 2.

Goal 3.

THREE-MONTH STRATEGIES OR ACTIVITIES TO ACHIEVE MY GOALS

Goal 1:

A.

B.

C.

Goal 2:

A.

B.

C.

Goal 3:

A.

B.

C.

ONE-YEAR GOALS

Goal 1.

Goal 2.

Goal 3.

ONE-YEAR STRATEGIES OR ACTIVITIES TO ACHIEVE MY GOALS

Goal 1:

A.

B.

C.

Goal 2:

A.

B.

C.

Goal 3:

A.

B.

C.

LIFETIME GOALS

Goal 1.

Goal 2.

Goal 3.

LIFETIME STRATEGIES OR ACTIVITIES TO ACHIEVE MY GOALS:

Goal 1:

A.

B.

C.

Goal 2:

A.

B.

C.

Goal 3:

A.

B.

C.

Exhibit 2: MY TIME LOG

TIME	Heading	Heading	Heading	Heading	Heading	Heading	Heading	Heading
6:00								
6:30								
7:00								
7:30								
8:00								
8:30								
9:00								
9:30								
10:00								
10:30								
11:00								
11:30								
12:00								
12:30								
1:00								
1:30								
2:00								
2:30								
3:00								

Appendix — Exhibit 2

TIME	Heading	Heading	Heading	Heading	Heading	Heading	Heading	Heading
3:30								
4:00								
4:30								
5:00								
5:30								
6:00								
6:30								
7:00								
7:30								
8:00								
8:30								
9:00								
9:30								
10:00								
10:30								
11:00								
11:30								
12:00								

Instructions:

1. Select a name for each Column heading, e.g., prayer, meals, exercise, etc.
2. Insert an "x" for each 10 minutes spent within each 1/2 hour category.

For example: If you spend 20 minutes from 6:30 to 6:50 in morning prayer and another 10 minutes in physical exercise, you would indicate 2 "x" marks in the prayer box and one "x" in the personal box. Many people work during the hours of 8 A.M. to 5 P.M., hence half-hour periods are used.

A sample partially completed Time Log follows:

Time	Prayer	Ministry	Meals	Family	Social	Personal	Unaccounted	Comments
6:00	xx					x		
6:30			xx	x				
7:00		xx				x		
7:30		xx				x		
8:00	xxx							
8:30		xxx						
9:00			x		x		x	

Exhibit 3
TYPICAL TIME-WASTERS

Self-Imposed Time-Wasters

1. Procrastination and indecision
2. Poor planning and organization
3. Trying to do too many things at one time
4. Unrealistic time estimates
5. Doing everything yourself
6. Can't say "No"
7. Failure to listen carefully
8. Delegating authority without accountability
9. Involving too many people
10. Refusing to let others do the job
11. Bypassing the chain of command
12. Snap decisions
13. Placing blame on others
14. Majoring in minors
15. Fear of failure and consequences of possible mistakes
16. Day-dreaming
17. Excessive socializing
18. Letting others put their "monkey" on your back
19. Reacting to the "urgent" rather than the most important
20. Fatigue due to poor physical condition
21. Duplicating your efforts
22. Inadequate motivation
23. Unrealistic optimism
24. "Telephonitis" and "Computeritis"
25. Too much attention to minute details
26. Leaving too many projects unfinished
27. Disorganized desk, files, books, etc.
28. No daily "to-do" list or plan of action

Externally Imposed Time-Wasters

1. Meetings
2. Telephone
3. Television, snail-mail, & e-mail
4. Chit-Chat
5. Interruptions
6. Poor communication
7. Inadequate information
8. Lack of delegation by superiors
9. Parishioners with petty problems
10. Lack of priorities by others
11. Mistakes of others
12. Routine maintenance chores
13. Unavailability of assistance
14. Unexpected jobs
15. Others' delays, tardiness, and failure to follow through

Exhibit 4
DAILY TO-DO LIST FOR GOD

Daily Spiritual Activities (related to my Spiritual Goal 1.)

Activity 1. _____

Activity 2. _____

Activity 3. _____

Daily Spiritual Activities (related to my Spiritual Goal 2.)

Activity 1. _____

Activity 2. _____

Activity 3. _____

Daily Spiritual Activities (related to my Spiritual Goal 3.)

Activity 1. _____

Activity 2. _____

Activity 3. _____

➤ Your Daily Spiritual Activities, for the most part, should relate to your Spiritual Goals, and strategies to achieve them, which you identified in Exhibit 1.

➤ You may wish to maintain this Daily To-Do List for God as a separate daily activity list, or incorporate these activities into a general To-Do List in which you would normally include the activities for all other areas of your life, including your personal and professional, family and home, and other areas of responsibility and obligation.

Exhibit 5
HOW TO CONDUCT EFFECTIVE AND EFFICIENT MEETINGS

What To Do Prior To A Meeting

1. Identify possible alternate approaches.
   Ask yourself and proposed invitees:
   "Is this meeting really necessary?"
   "Can we achieve our objectives through other methods: teleconference, memos, e-mails, etc.?"
   "Can the agenda be combined with another function?"
   "Should I delegate another representative to act on my behalf?"

2. Identify clearly the objectives of the meeting; write them down and be specific about them when inviting attendees.

3. Specify the amount of time you can attend.

4. Select the optimum time. Schedule meeting before or after another function, e.g., church services or other related events.

5. Be firm in limiting the number who absolutely need to attend.

6. Select a suitable facility and location convenient for the majority.

7. Circulate the agenda before the meeting. Set a time limit for the meeting and the respective topics in their order of importance.

What To Do During The Meeting

1. Pray that the Holy Spirit will grant the gifts of Wisdom and Knowledge.
2. Start on time. Be ruthless with yourself and firm with others. Appoint a secretary and timekeeper.
3. State the meeting objectives, follow the agenda, and insist on time limits for each topic.
4. Be in command. Control interruptions, detours, etc. Don't tolerate sidebar discussions.
5. Be certain you achieve the objectives of the meeting.
6. Summarize the decisions, responsibilities, and deadlines so that all attendees are in agreement. Record them on the Meeting Summary.
7. Conclude at the agreed-upon time.

When the Meeting Is Over

1. Circulate printed copies of meeting minutes to all attendees within 3-4 days. This is of utmost importance since it reinforces the effectiveness of the meeting.
2. Follow-up with attendees to make sure they have performed the actions they've promised.
3. Save the meeting summaries for future reference. They will help you recall the decisions made on issues which may surface again.

Exhibit 6
MEETING MINUTES SUMMARY

Date_____

Name of Group_____ Subject _____

Persons Attending_____

Decisions	Person Responsible	Action	Deadline	Follow-Up Results
1)				
2)				
3)				
4)				
5)				
6)				
7)				
8)				
9)				

BIBLIOGRAPHY

The author has endeavored to credit all known persons holding copyrights or reproduction rights for passages quoted in this book.

Introduction

Murnion, Philip J. and David DeLambo. *Parishes and Parish Ministries: A Study of Lay Ministry*. New York: The National Pastoral Life Center, 1999.

Chapter 1

Montaigne, Michel de. *The Complete Essays of Montaigne*. New York: Penguin Classics, 1991.

Chapter 2

Covey, Stephen. *The 8th Habit – From Effectiveness to Greatness*. New York: Simon & Schuster, 2004.

Greenleaf, Robert. *The Institution as Servant*. Frankfort, MI: The Robert K. Greenleaf Center for Servant-Leadership, 1976.

Shakespeare, William. *The Complete Works of Shakespeare*. New York: Garden City Publishing Co., 1936.

Chapter 3

Burle, Sr. Marie, C.P.P.S. and Sr. Sharon Plankenhorn, *You Will Receive Power*. Pecos, NM: Dove Publications, 1977.

Holmes, Oliver Wendell. *The One Hoss Shay: The Deacon's Masterpiece.* From *The Poetical Works of Holmes,* New York: Houghton Mifflin Co., 1990.

McManimon, James P. *Conference Address to Deacons.* Diocese of Trenton, NJ, 1980.

Meissner, W.W., S.J. *Ignatius of Loyola: The Psychology of a Saint.* New Haven, CT: Yale University Press, 1992.

Murnion, Philip J. and Frank J. McNulty. *Keeping All In Balance.* New York: The National Pastoral Life Center, 2000.

Chapter 4

Murnion, Philip J. ibid.

Zubik, Most Rev. David A., Bishop, Diocese of Green Bay, WI. *Keynote Address NACPA Convocation,* Orlando, 2002.

Chapter 6

Peale, Norman Vincent. *Imaging: The Powerful Way to Change Your Life.* New York: Fleming H. Revell Co., 1982.

Chapter 7

Robinson, John R. *How Americans Spend Time.* (out of print)

Chapter 8

Bliss, Edwin. *Getting Things Done: The A B C's of Time Management.* New York: Charles Scribners and Sons, 1976.

Hartman, Msgr. Thomas J. *Interview with Archbishop Fulton J. Sheen.* New York, 1987.

Mackenzie, Dr. Alec R. *The Time Trap.* New York, 1987.

Sweetser, Fr. Thomas P., S.J. *The Parish as Covenant – A Call to*

Pastoral Partnership. Lanham, MD: Sheed and Ward, 2001.

Chapter 9

Scanlan, Fr. Michael, T.O.R. *What Does God Want: A Practical Guide for Making Decisions.* Huntington, IN: Our Sunday Visitor, 1996.

Thompson, Francis. *The Hound of Heaven.* From *Poems,* Volume I, 1913. Charles Scribner's Sons. London: Burns & Oates Ltd.

Chapter 10

Ford, Fr. Michael. *Fr. Mychal Judge – An Authentic American Hero.* Mahwah, NJ: Paulist Press, 2002.

Kelly, Matthew. *The Rhythm of Life.* Steubenville, OH: Beacon Publishing, 1999.

Martin, Ralph. *Unless the Lord Build the House – The Church and the New Pentecost.* Notre Dame, IN: Ave Maria Press, 1971.

Maynard, Rev. Dennis. Article in *The Anglican Digest –* Transfiguration, Houston, TX, November 1997.

Odiorne, George. *Avoid the Activity Trap.* New York: Harper Collins Publishers, Inc., 1970.

Chapter 13

Brother Lawrence of the Resurrection. *The Practice of the Presence of God – Conversations and Letters of Nicholas Hermann of Lorraine.* Old Tappan, NJ: A Spire Book. Jove Publications for Fleming H. Revell Co., 1958.

Sheen, Archbishop Fulton J. *Those Mysterious Priests.* Garden City, NY: Doubleday & Co., 1974.

Biography

John Flanagan was ordained a Permanent Deacon for the Diocese of Trenton, New Jersey in May 1981 and has served since then at St. Catharine Church, Holmdel, New Jersey. For several years he was the Director of Stewardship for the Diocese of Trenton and lectured extensively on Stewardship and management topics. As President of his own consulting company, Catholic Church Campaigns, located in New Jersey, John conducted hundreds of Stewardship and Capital Building campaigns in the New Jersey and New York Dioceses.

John retired as Vice President, Administration for Prudential Insurance Company's subsidiary, Prudential Property & Casualty Co., and was the former President of Management Seminars, a marketing Company in New York City.

Mr. Flanagan has contributed articles to both the religious and secular media.

John and his wife Eileen reside in Red Bank, New Jersey and are the parents of five children.